What People Are Saying

M000107605

This exceptional work by Dr. Joshua Fowler is one of the most profound yet practical approaches to this subject of praise and worship that I have read in a long time. The author's approach to this timely issue is a fresh breath of air that captivates the heart, engages the mind, and inspires the spirit. *Prophetic Praise* is a gift of motivation to worship.

—*Dr. Myles Munroe*
Best-selling author; president and founder,
Bahamas Faith Ministries International
Nassau, Bahamas

Joshua Fowler is a man of God in passionate pursuit of His presence, and has been since he was a teenager. His breadth and depth of understanding regarding the heart of the Father, and what He is seeking from His sons and daughters, is drawn from his wealth of study and his handling of the Word of God for many, many years. He is a seasoned apostolic voice with a fresh mandate to unleash a flood tide of God's glorious river in and through the saints. *Prophetic Praise* is a hands-on, lifelong learning manual describing where the move of God needs to be directed and flowing in the coming days.

—*Dr. Mark J. Chironna*
Senior Pastor, The Master's Touch International Church
Orlando, Florida

In *Prophetic Praise*, you will be inspired to live life from the heavenlies, and see God's kingdom demonstrated in the earth. Dr. Joshua Fowler has written a book that will equip you to rule and reign from God's seat of authority, as you walk in the revelation of being seated in heavenly places in Christ. There is a sound of praise waiting to be released through you. As it is released, not only will your own prison doors open, but God will make you a point of breakthrough for others, as well. Get ready to rule over your enemies as God's praise marks your life.

—*Matt Sorger*
President, Matt Sorger Ministries/television host, *Power for Life*
Seldon, New York

Prophetic Praise is a timely written work of revelation that will elevate every believer into a life that will establish the reign of Christ in their everyday lives. Apostle Fowler is a modern-day David, who will help you to release the sounds of heaven into your own life, resulting in a manifestation of the presence of God that will heal, restore, and refresh the heart of the worshipper.

—*Tammy Chism*
Impact Life Centre
Tulsa, Oklahoma

Dr. Fowler has written a true gem with *Prophetic Praise*. I would highly recommend it to anyone who desires a greater understanding of what truly happens when we release the sound of praise. I am convinced that these concepts and teachings can truly unlock our authority in the kingdom, as well as change the way we approach our corporate and personal times of worship. This is a must-read!

—*Trent Cory*
Minister, worship leader, and songwriter

In his book *Prophetic Praise*, Joshua Fowler brings a renewed understanding of the purpose and power of praise to the twenty-first-century church. His passion to see the body of Christ understand and embrace their position, seated in heavenly places with Christ, will stir you to take your place as a governor of praise on the earth. Allow the truths in this book to penetrate your heart and transform your expressions of praise into prophetic decrees that shatter the enemy's territory and release the kingdom of God!

—*Kelanie Gloeckler*
Songwriter and worship leader, New Life Christian Fellowship
Jacksonville, Florida

Joshua Fowler has written a book that is a must-read for every believer, especially pastors. I had the amazing privilege of reading *Prophetic Praise* while ministering in worship gatherings across the nation Brazil. It stirred my faith and stoked the flame in my heart to see a nation changed through the power of praise! The revelation in this book is crucial for the times in which we are living. There is an urgency in this hour for the children of God to step into a place of authority in our worship! I know Joshua Fowler personally and have ministered in his church for years. He lives what he teaches in this book. I wholeheartedly, and without reservation, recommend *Prophetic Praise*. It will challenge you and hopefully bring some new insight to the way you view the power of your praise!

—*Jason Lee Jones*
Worship recording artist
Savannah, Georgia

Apostle Joshua has a calling to lead the body of Christ into the presence of the Lord; he is gifted in this way. His new book, *Prophetic Praise*, will bring you into a new dimension in praise. When I first met Joshua at a conference, the Lord gave me a word for him: that, as a drummer, he carries the heart of God, which is released as he plays the drums. He releases the heartbeat of God for praise. Your life will never be the same as you engage in the revelation he shares in this book.

—*Apostle Mark van Gundy*
Senior Pastor, Church of Destiny and Igreja Philadelphia
London, England

Joshua Fowler is a voice to this generation. God has raised this man up as a general. *Prophetic Praise* is a must-read. As the church continues to understand the power behind our praise, we will take territory for His kingdom. In this book, you will get an understanding of prophetic praise. Prophetic praise is not praising God for something that has already happened; it's praising God for something to happen. Apostle Fowler, you did it again!

—*J. R. Gonzalez*
Senior Pastor, Dominion Life Center
North Hollywood, California

Apostle Joshua has truly heard from God in writing *Prophetic Praise*! In an age when people are collectively spending millions on conferences and retreats to find the "outpouring" of God's presence, Apostle Joshua has brought us back to our original purpose of worshipping God, taking dominion on earth, and thus finding His "outpouring"!

—Apostle Steve Perea
West Coast FiveFold Network
Manteca, California

When I began reading this book, the image that came to mind was of holding a "tuning fork" in your hands. I believe that's what this book will do for your life. I believe the revelation of praise and worship is a tuning fork that brings us into unity with God and into His very manifest love and presence. I encourage you to open your heart, mind, and spirit to embrace the journey of revelation that Joshua Fowler embarks upon in this book. In your hands are some precious keys of revelation that will take you deeper in your walk with Jesus Christ!

—*Ryan Wyatt*
Founding lead pastor, Fuse Church
Knoxville, Tennessee

It is with great pleasure that I take this opportunity to endorse *Prophetic Praise*. Having known Dr. Fowler for more than twelve years, I know that what is contained in the pages of this book is from a man who operates in true prophetic praise. I highly recommend this book, not only to church leaders but also to laypeople everywhere who seriously desire to be grounded in an understanding of praise and worship. Read, then go forth in *Prophetic Praise*!

—*Michael Scantlebury*
Author and founding apostle, Kingdom-Impact International Network

Prophetic Praise by Joshua Fowler provides a real solution for those who have been called to take territories for the kingdom of God. It is authentic, insightful, and replete with useful strategies for releasing the power of praise in any situation. In my work as a life-change strategist, I will, without a doubt, put this tool in the hands of those individuals, teams, and organizations who desire to realize their God-given right to take dominion. Every kingdom practitioner should have a copy in his arsenal.

—*Dr. Michael A. Phillips*
Certified Business Advisor and senior leader,
Kingdom Life International Center
Orlando, Florida

PROPHETIC
PRAISE

PROPHETIC
PRAISE

JOSHUA
FOWLER

WHITAKER
HOUSE

Unless otherwise indicated, all Scripture quotations are taken from the *New King James Version*, © 1979, 1980, 1982, 1984 by Thomas Nelson, Inc. Used by permission. All rights reserved. Scripture quotations marked (NIV) are taken from the *Holy Bible, New International Version*®, NIV®, © 1973, 1978, 1984 by the International Bible Society. Used by permission of Zondervan. All rights reserved. Scripture quotations marked (KJV) are taken from the King James Version of the Holy Bible. Scripture quotations marked (MSG) are taken from *The Message: The Bible in Contemporary Language* by Eugene H. Peterson, © 1993, 1994, 1995, 1996, 2000, 2001, 2002. Used by permission of NavPress Publishing Group. All rights reserved. Scripture quotations marked (AMP) are taken from the *Amplified*® *Bible*, © 1954, 1958, 1962, 1964, 1965, 1987 by The Lockman Foundation. Used by permission. (www.Lockman.org). Scripture quotations marked (NASB) are taken from the updated *New American Standard Bible*®, NASB®, © 1960, 1962, 1963, 1968, 1971, 1972, 1973, 1975, 1977, 1995 by The Lockman Foundation. Used by permission. (www.Lockman.org). Scripture quotation marked (NLT) is taken from the *Holy Bible, New Living Translation*, © 1996, 2004, 2007. Used by permission of Tyndale House Publishers, Inc., Carol Stream, Illinois 60188. All rights reserved.

Publisher's Notes: The name satan, and related names, are not capitalized. We choose not to acknowledge him, even to the point of violating grammatical rules. Bold text in Scripture quotations signifies the emphasis of the author.

Some definitions of words are taken from *Merriam-Webster's 11ᵗʰ Collegiate Dictionary.* Some definitions of Hebrew and Greek words are taken from the electronic versions of *Strong's Exhaustive Concordance of the Bible* (© 1980, 1986, and assigned to World Bible Publishers, Inc. All rights reserved).

PROPHETIC PRAISE:
Upload Worship, Download Heaven
(Originally published under the title *Governors of Praise*)

Joshua Fowler
www.joshuafowler.com

ISBN: 978-1-60374-953-4 • eBook ISBN: 978-1-60374-978-7
Printed in the United States of America
© 2012, 2014 by Joshua Fowler

Whitaker House
1030 Hunt Valley Circle
New Kensington, PA 15068
www.whitakerhouse.com

Library of Congress Cataloging-in-Publication Data (Pending)

No part of this book may be reproduced or transmitted in any form or by any means, electronic or mechanical—including photocopying, recording, or by any information storage and retrieval system—without permission in writing from the publisher. Please direct your inquiries to permissionseditor@whitakerhouse.com.

1 2 3 4 5 6 7 8 9 10 ᴜᴊ 21 20 19 18 17 16 15 14

CONTENTS

FOREWORD

I have personally seen Joshua Fowler's passion for praise, worship, and the presence of God. His passion for worship is evident in his local church and can be seen in the people he has raised up to be true worshippers. His passion can also be seen in this book. The revelation in *Prophetic Praise* is necessary for those who want to have significant breakthroughs in their personal lives, ministries, and territories.

There is an authority and power that is released through praise; this is what the book is about. Praise is a weapon, and praise is a part of ruling and reigning with Christ. Jesus comes from the tribe of Judah. The scepter comes from the tribe of Judah. God's tabernacle was in Judah. His presence was in Zion, which was located in Judah. "Praisers" have the spiritual DNA of Judah, the tribe from which Christ the Ruler comes. It is more necessary than ever that leaders teach on the subject of praise. God inhabits the praises of Israel. (See Psalm 22:3 KJV.) In other words, praise brings the presence of God; the King dwells in the midst of praise. This book will challenge readers to see the importance of praise for today's church. As Joshua says, "Praise is not a preliminary part of the church service."

Praise among the nations was God's ultimate plan and purpose through the redemptive act of Christ's death and sacrifice. The Lord's directive to Joshua—"Teach My people to worship Me, for worship is the closest place on earth to Me"—is the motivation for this book. God is pleased when people are taught to worship.

As you read this book, allow the inspired words to settle in your spirit. Joshua writes from a place of prophetic authority and revelation. This is not an echo of what has been written before. There is always fresh revelation for a new generation, and Joshua is a voice to this generation. His assignment is to see a new generation arise and come forth in praise and worship that will go further than that of previous generations. We have yet to see the fullness of what God desires to do through *Prophetic Praise*. The best is yet to come. There are miracles that are yet to be released. Get ready to go on a new journey in praise.

—*John Eckhardt*
Apostle and overseer, Crusaders Church Chicago
Chicago, Illinois

INTRODUCTION

It was in an obscure place nestled in the middle of what appeared to be "Nowhereville." As a mere sixteen-year-old, I had a God encounter that shook me to my core and unleashed an insatiable appetite for the presence of God. This encounter didn't happen at a large conference or in a megachurch. It didn't happen with world-renowned speakers or worship teams. It took place in a small church on the frozen farmlands of Wisconsin.

I had never witnessed anything like it before. The atmosphere was pregnant with expectancy and fueled by intense hunger and prayer. Throughout the day, people were coming continuously on their breaks to walk the floors of the sanctuary, praying and singing in the Spirit. The church had a private school, and every hour, the students would open the classroom doors and fall on their faces, praying and singing in the Spirit. When it came time for the service, the atmosphere was so thick with the presence of God that you could have cut it with a knife! The people were not satisfied with the typical "little dab will do" song service but pressed in with passion until they touched the Lord.

After the Word was preached, many people came forward, giving their lives to the Lord. Instead of closing with a few remarks and prayer, the pastor called for the worship team and commanded the people to enter in with the angels who were rejoicing over the souls that were saved. Like a volcano, the place erupted with shouting, dancing, and singing. In the midst of this, I closed my eyes, lifted my hands, let go, and began to dance. Suddenly, it was as if I had been raptured into higher realms of praise and worship than I had ever experienced before. Although I had started out seven rows back, I was oblivious to the fact that I praised my way to the front of the sanctuary, beside the keyboard. The song ended with a crescendo, and the pastor began addressing the people.

Although I tried to restrain myself, I was drunk on the "new wine" and couldn't stop laughing. The pastor and the church heard me and joined me in laughter. My emotions overflowed, and I began to weep tears of joy. I fell to my knees, and when I touched the floor, heaven opened, and I heard the most beautiful sounds I have ever heard! It was the host of heaven worshipping before God's throne. Then the Lord said something that would send me on the quest that has shaped my life's destiny. He said, "Teach My people to worship Me, for worship is the closest place to Me on earth." By this point, I was weeping and trembling uncontrollably. Then, I heard a loud *boom*! It was the jarring sound of the cordless microphone as Pastor John jumped off the platform and ran over to me. He placed his hand on my head and released a prophecy that still resounds in my spirit today: "I have put My Word in your mouth and a stone in your hand to set this generation free."

I believe this book is part of the fulfillment of that prophecy: a word and a stone to set generations free. As you read it, it is my desire that you will be stirred to a greater hunger and passion for the Lord, and that you will enter into the realm of prophetic praise.

In this book, you will discover that when you "upload" praise and worship to the heavens, it draws the lost into the kingdom and "downloads" heaven, releasing signs and wonders and allowing us to spiritually govern territories and impact nations for Christ! Move beyond the revelation, receive the impartation, and, when the Holy Spirit moves upon your heart, enter into participation! Whether you kneel, lift your hands, sing, dance, shout, cry, or laugh, let yourself go and join heaven's host in the realm of prophetic praise.

1

UPLOAD WORSHIP

believe Isaiah 55 is a master key to understanding how to download heaven. This passage has made an indelible mark upon my life. I don't share this to boast, but it has become so real in my life that it seems to fall out of my Bible and wash over me. In fact, the entire book of Isaiah rains over my life and prophesies to me all the time. These words were penned centuries ago, but they are more fresh and real today than ever before.

Isaiah 55: A Master Key

"Ho! Everyone who thirsts, come to the waters; and you who have no money, come, buy and eat. Yes, come, buy wine and milk without money and without price. Why do you spend money for what is not bread, and your wages for what does not satisfy? Listen carefully to Me, and eat what is good, and let your soul delight itself in abundance. Incline your ear, and come to Me. Hear, and your soul shall live; and I will make an everlasting covenant with you—the sure mercies of

David. Indeed I have given him as a witness to the people, a leader and commander for the people. Surely you shall call a nation you do not know, and nations who do not know you shall run to you, because of the LORD *your God, and the Holy One of Israel; for He has glorified you. Seek the* LORD *while He may be found, call upon Him while He is near. Let the wicked forsake his way, and the unrighteous man his thoughts; let him return to the* LORD, *and He will have mercy on him; and to our God, for He will abundantly pardon. For My thoughts are not your thoughts, nor are your ways My ways," says the* LORD. *"For as the heavens are higher than the earth, so are My ways higher than your ways, and My thoughts than your thoughts. For as the rain comes down, and the snow from heaven, and do not return there, but water the earth, and make it bring forth and bud, that it may give seed to the sower and bread to the eater, so shall My word be that goes forth from My mouth; it shall not return to Me void, but it shall accomplish what I please, and it shall prosper in the thing for which I sent it. For you shall go out with joy, and be led out with peace; the mountains and the hills shall break forth into singing before you, and all the trees of the field shall clap their hands. Instead of the thorn shall come up the cypress tree, and instead of the brier shall come up the myrtle tree; and it shall be to the* LORD *for a name, for an everlasting sign that shall not be cut off."*

(Isaiah 55)

My Water Is Worship

My water is worship, and heaven's rain is my life's sustenance. Heaven's rain is everything I need. So, when I offer worship, it goes up in a form of water to refresh my Father God. But, when He sends it back down as rain, within it is whatever I need.

For as the rain comes down, and the snow from heaven, and do not return there, but water the earth, and make it bring forth and bud, that it may give seed to the sower and bread to the eater, so shall My word be that goes forth from My mouth; it shall not return to Me void, but it shall accomplish what I please, and it shall prosper in the thing for which I sent it. (Isaiah 55:10–11)

Rain isn't created in the sky. It is drawn up into the heavens from the earth in the form of evaporation. The barometric pressure begins to fall, pulling up the moisture from the oceans, lakes, and other bodies of water, into the heavens. This water rises up from the earth in one form— vapor—but when it comes back down, it is released in a new form—rain!

In Isaiah 55, God is giving us a key! *"For as the rain comes down and the snow from heaven, and do not return there, but water the earth, and make it bring forth and bud, that it may give seed to the sower and bread to the eater, so shall My word be that goes forth from My mouth."*

We are God's body on earth. If He is going to speak, He is going to speak through us. If He is going to move, He is going to move on the earth through us. All across the planet, God is looking for people who will get His Word into their mouths so that it might be released—those who will send His Word into the heavens through praise and worship. Like water, as we worship the Lord, it goes up in one form, but it does not return unto Him void. It will accomplish whatever it was sent to accomplish.

If you need to see a breakthrough in your finances, begin to worship *Jehovah Jireh*—"The Lord your Provider"! As you lift Him up, guess what comes back down? The rain of supernatural increase.

If you need healing, worship *Jehovah Rafeh*—"God heals"! The more you worship, saying, "You are my healer," guess what happens? Healing rains down! As you send the right thing up, the right thing will come back down, because what goes up must come down. As you upload worship, the thing for which you are believing will manifest.

So [Jesus] came to a city of Samaria which is called Sychar, near the plot of ground that Jacob gave to his son Joseph. Now Jacob's well was there. Jesus therefore, being wearied from His journey, sat thus by the well. It was about the sixth hour. A woman of Samaria came to draw water. Jesus said to her, "Give Me a drink." For His disciples had gone away into the city to buy food. Then the woman of Samaria said to Him, "How is it that You, being a Jew, ask a drink from me, a Samaritan woman?" For Jews have no dealings with Samaritans. Jesus answered and said to her, "If you knew the gift of God, and who it is who says to you, 'Give Me a drink,' you would have asked Him, and He would have given you living water." The woman said to Him, "Sir, You have nothing to draw with, and the well is deep. Where then do You get that living water? Are You greater than our father Jacob, who gave us the well, and drank from it himself, as well as his sons and his livestock?" Jesus answered and said to her, "Whoever drinks of this water will thirst again, but whoever drinks of the water that I shall give him will never thirst. But the water that I shall give him will become in him a fountain of water springing up into everlasting life." The woman said to Him, "Sir, give me this water, that I may not thirst, nor come here to draw." Jesus said to her, "Go, call your husband, and come here." The woman answered and said, "I have no husband." Jesus said to her, "You have well said, 'I have no husband,' for you have had five husbands, and the one whom you now have is not your husband; in that you spoke truly." The woman said to Him, "Sir, I perceive that You are a prophet. Our fathers worshipped on this mountain, and you Jews say that in Jerusalem is the place where one ought to worship." Jesus said to her, "Woman, believe Me, the hour is coming when you will neither on this mountain, nor in Jerusalem, worship the Father. You worship what you do not know; we know what we worship, for salvation is of the Jews. But the hour is coming, and now is, when the true worshippers will worship the Father in spirit and truth; for the Father is seeking such to worship Him. God is Spirit, and those who worship Him must worship in spirit and truth." The woman said to Him, "I know that Messiah is coming" (who is called Christ). "When He comes, He will tell us all things."

(John 4:5–25)

I can just imagine Jesus sitting on the well. You might say that "the Well" was sitting on the well! When the Samaritan woman came up to him, He asked her to get Him a drink. Then He revealed a powerful insight into the water of worship. You see, Jesus chose to use this well to illustrate how worship is connected to water.

Jesus is still thirsty today, and He's searching for people who will bring Him a refreshing drink of water from the wells of worship. Like the Samaritan woman, many people today are still distracted by *where* they should worship and *with whom* they should worship. Jesus broke it down: Our worship should never be confined to a place; worship is not something we do only on Sundays at church. It is not the warm-up band for the sermon. Worship is a lifestyle. Worship is a poured-out, 24/7 lifestyle. Worship is a perpetual drink offering submitted unto the Lord. The Father is still seeking true worshippers today—those who will worship Him in spirit and truth. Before you read any further, take this opportunity to offer up your life to the Father as a drink offering. Pour your worship on Him. Let Him know how much you love Him. Sing a new song of praise and worship to the Lord.

The U.P.L.O.A.D.

U = Uprightness

Who may ascend into the hill of the LORD? Or who may stand in His holy place? He who has clean hands and a pure heart, who has not lifted up his soul to an idol, nor sworn deceitfully. (Psalm 24:3–4)

Give unto the LORD the glory due to His name; worship the LORD in the beauty of holiness. (Psalm 29:2)

Pure worship must originate from the beauty of holiness. Only upright people can release uploads of praise and worship. I may not understand how the Internet works, but I'm glad it does! With one click of my computer mouse, I can send an e-mail to the other side of the world. That's amazing! I can Skype with someone who lives in a far-off country. Of course, making those connections depends on having an unblocked transmission and plenty of signal strength. If the antenna of your Wi-Fi modem is obstructed or out of position, your computer will not be able to go online.

Likewise, with worship, there are many Christians who are not able to receive a strong signal from heaven because they're not living upright lives. God wants to make you upright! He wants to restore you to a place of righteousness.

Have you seen the movie *Up*? In it, the main character attaches a huge number of helium balloons to his house, and it flies up, up, and away! It floats off to the place where his dear, departed wife always wanted it to go. There are a lot of people who never rise up, because they don't have the "helium" of an upright spirit.

True worship is not horizontal; it's vertical. True worship is upward. Would you like to experience upward mobility? Would you like to receive a promotion? The Bible says that promotion comes from the Lord. (See Psalm 75:6–7 KJV.) So, if you want promotion in any area of your life, you have to look upward. Rubbing shoulders with people here on the earth won't get you the upward mobility you expect. You must "rub shoulders" with God; you must lay your head on His chest! When you spend time with Him, upward mobility is inevitable!

P = Passion

We must be a passionate people of prayer, praise, and prophecy if we expect to be able to upload praise. Have you ever eaten something that looked good on the outside, only to find, when you took that first bite, that it hadn't been fully cooked? Wasn't that frustrating? Half-baked praise is thoughtless praise. Don't allow your praise to be an afterthought. Be passionate! You don't pay good money to see a movie you expect to depress you. You go to a movie because you want to be inspired—you want to have your soul lifted; you want to see someone get excited about something. You don't go to a ball game to see your favorite team go through the motions and lose. You want your team to put it all on the line and win! You want to experience passion in your life!

Your worship of God should be both intimate and passionate. This is what the Lord desires of you. It is what makes your relationship with Him work. If your relationship with God is scheduled only on Sundays, it won't work. God desires to be intimately woven throughout all the areas of your life. He wants to be involved in what you do, what you say, and where you go. He wants to be your first thought when you awake in the morning and your last thought before you drift off to sleep at night. That is passion, and it is vital to your relationship with God!

It's a shame the way some people treat God. They say, "I saw Him last week at church. We're doing great. I threw some money in the bucket, so I'm good."

No! God is not your weekend date. Don't treat Him like a person of ill-repute at whom you throw money for a good time. Sorry to be crude, but that is how some people treat God. You're supposed to be in covenant with Him, in love with Him, spending time with Him. It needs to be passionate. You have to say, "What can I do for You, God? How can I show You my love?" God knows what you desire, and He wants to lavish His affection on you.

Do you know what God wants? What He needs? He wants your worship.

My wife likes receiving love notes. I leave them for her on the refrigerator. The first thing she sees in the morning is a note telling her how beautiful she is and how much I love her. She needs to feel that she is loved. She also knows that I need her to show me affection, as well. She does that for me. We constantly communicate with each other in order to express our passion and love. I'm not saying that we are perfect, but I am saying that this is how it works in a relationship, and this is how it should work with your relationship with God.

*A religion scholar stood up with a question to test Jesus. "Teacher, what do I need to do to get eternal life?" He answered, "What's written in God's Law? How do you interpret it?" He said, "That you love the Lord your God with all your **passion** and prayer and muscle and intel-*

ligence—and that you love your neighbor as well as you do yourself."
(Luke 10:25–27 MSG)

[God said,] "But my servant Caleb—this is a different story. He has a different spirit; he follows me **passionately***. I'll bring him into the land that he scouted and his children will inherit it."*
(Numbers 14:24 MSG)

God proves to be good to the man who **passionately** *waits, to the woman who diligently seeks.* (Lamentations 3:25 MSG)

There's more to come: We continue to shout our praise even when we're hemmed in with troubles, because we know how troubles can develop **passionate** *patience in us.* (Romans 5:3 MSG)

You do so well in so many things—you trust God, you're articulate, you're insightful, you're **passionate***, you love us—now, do your best in this, too.* (2 Corinthians 8:7 MSG)

Because you kept my Word in **passionate** *patience, I'll keep you safe in the time of testing….* (Revelation 3:10 MSG)

Wait **passionately** *for God, don't leave the path. He'll give you your place in the sun while you watch the wicked lose it.*
(Psalm 37:34 MSG)

One day as they were **worshipping** *God—they were also fasting as they waited for guidance—the Holy Spirit spoke: "Take Barnabas and Saul and commission them for the work I have called them to do." So they commissioned them. In that* **circle of intensity** *and obedience, of fasting and praying, they laid hands on their heads and sent them* *off. Sent off on their new assignment by the Holy Spirit, Barnabas and Saul went down to Seleucia and caught a ship for Cyprus.*

(Acts 13:2–4 MSG)

If you want to increase in passionate, prophetic praise and worship, there are some powerful keys nestled within Acts 13:2–4. I have been in ministry all of my adult life and have preached the gospel for more than twenty-five years. I've taught numerous times on truths from Acts 13, but recently, I was reading Acts 13 in *The Message* Bible when I noticed something I'd never seen before. I had always taught about the steps toward the commissioning of Barnabas and Saul—worship, prayer, fasting, and the Holy Spirit speaking through the prophets—but what leapt off the page and into my spirit were three words: *"circle of intensity."* When I read those words, I recognized a missing ingredient in the lives of many believers and churches.

Imagine life in the book of Acts. Imagine what it was like to experience such passion and intensity with believers who hadn't bought into the lies of convenient and complaisant Christianity. Those apostles and disciples worshipped, fasted, and prayed as if their lives depended on it. Why? Because their lives really did depend on it. They were facing persecution, prison, death threats, and the risk of seeing their loved ones murdered because of their allegiance to Christ. Most of us aren't faced with such threats today, but we should still worship, fast, and pray as if our lives depend on it. Every believer needs to be a part of a "circle of intensity" of at least two or three other brothers or sisters in Christ, a group of individuals who hold each other accountable and encourage one another to pursue the Lord with passion.

It's always easier to get through a workout if you have someone else spotting and encouraging you as you lift weights or run. We need someone else to say, "You've got this; you can do it; you can lift it one more time; you can run one more mile." We all need someone who will call us and say, "Get off that couch and meet me at the gym!" We all need someone who, from time to time, will get in our face and urge us to do good works. So it is with this passionate pursuit of God. We need a circle of intensity—a group of fellow believers who will encourage us by saying, "God's got this; keep pressing into Him; keep uploading worship and downloading heaven! You have one more song in you; you have a higher level of praise; now, reach for it!" We need someone who will call us and say, "Get off that couch, turn off that TV, and meet me at God's house for prayer and worship!"

Passion—how much do you have? Do you need more? If so, stop right now and ask the Lord to help you find your circle of intensity. As you receive names from the Lord, invite those individuals into your life. Ask them to be part of your circle of intensity. When you do this, you will experience passion like never before. From your circle of intensity, you and others will be commissioned into new assignments that will impact many lives for God's glory.

L = Lavishness

> Remember: A stingy planter gets a stingy crop; a **lavish** planter gets a **lavish** crop.　　　　　　　　　　　(2 Corinthians 9:6 MSG)

Live a lavish lifestyle of worship. Lavish your love on God! If you want to upload praise, you have to go overboard. Uploads don't happen on restricted lines of communication; that would take forever. Yet that is how many people live—on a weak signal. It's not lavish; it's not intense. If you want to make an intense breakthrough, you need intense worship. If you want an intense download of heaven—signs, wonders, and miracles, including the raising of the dead and the healing of the sick just by being in your shadow—you must display a lavish love of God. "I love You, God. I extol You; I magnify You. When I wake up, I magnify You!" That is what David would say. "Early in the morning, at noontime, and at night, I'm going to worship You." (See Psalm 55:17.)

Each day, we need to say, "What can I do for You, Jesus? How can I serve You today? How can I love You? I'll get that for You, God! I'll touch that person for You." That's an uploaded life. No matter what you are facing or going through, lavish your love on Him. Your heavenly Father lavished His love on you through the gift of His only begotten Son. Jesus lavished His love on you by laying down His life for you on the cross. God lavishly provides for you, every day. He lavishes you with compassion and extravagant love. If you want to lavish your love on the Lord, lay down your life through a lifestyle of lavish worship!

> These hard times are small potatoes compared to the coming good times, the **lavish** celebration prepared for us.
> (2 Corinthians 4:17 MSG)

> [God] wanted us to enter into the celebration of his **lavish** gift-giving by the hand of his beloved Son. (Ephesians 1:6 MSG)

> I'll make a list of GOD's gracious dealings, all the things GOD has done that need praising, all the generous bounties of GOD, his great goodness to the family of Israel—compassion lavished, love extravagant.
> (Isaiah 63:7 MSG)

> He never takes his eyes off the righteous; he honors them **lavishly**, promotes them endlessly. (Job 36:7 MSG)

> I will heal their waywardness. I will love them **lavishly**.
> (Hosea 14:4 MSG)

> Answer this question: Does the God who **lavishly** provides you with his own presence, his Holy Spirit, working things in your lives you could never do for yourselves, does he do these things because of your strenuous moral striving or because you trust him to do them in you?
> (Galatians 3:5 MSG)

> When God, who is the best shepherd of all, comes out in the open with his rule, he'll see that you've done it right and commend you **lavishly**.
> (1 Peter 5:4 MSG)

○ = Offering

"Now for the house of my God I have prepared with all my might: gold for things to be made of gold, silver for things of silver, bronze for things of bronze, iron for things of iron, wood for things of wood, onyx stones, stones to be set, glistening stones of various colors, all kinds of precious stones, and marble slabs in abundance. Moreover, because I have set my affection on the house of my God, I have given to the house of my God, over and above all that I have prepared for the holy house, my own special treasure of gold and silver: three thousand talents of gold, of the gold of Ophir, and seven thousand talents of refined silver, to overlay the walls of the houses; the gold for things of gold and the silver for things of silver, and for all kinds of work to be done by the hands of craftsmen. Who then is willing to consecrate himself this day to the LORD?" Then the leaders of the fathers' houses, leaders of the tribes of Israel, the captains of thousands and of hundreds, with the officers over the king's work, offered willingly. They gave for the work of the house of God five thousand talents and ten thousand darics of gold, ten thousand talents of silver, eighteen thousand talents of bronze, and one hundred thousand talents of iron. And whoever had precious stones gave them to the treasury of the house of the LORD, into the hand of Jehiel the Gershonite. Then the people rejoiced, for they had offered willingly, because with a loyal heart they had offered willingly to the LORD; and King David also rejoiced greatly.

(1 Chronicles 29:2–9)

Of all of the characters in the Bible, I would say that David would best personify what it means to be a true worshipper. David showed us by example that one of the primary ways to worship is through extravagant generosity. He led his family and the nation of Israel in giving the greatest offering ever recorded in history. If he were to make that offering today, it is estimated that the value would be $1,499,507,426! Now that's an offering! We should follow David's example and lavish our love on the Lord with extravagant offerings.

Remember: A stingy planter gets a stingy crop; a lavish planter gets a lavish crop. I want each of you to take plenty of time to think it over, and make up your own mind what you will give. That will protect you against sob stories and arm-twisting. God loves it when the giver delights in the giving. God can pour on the blessings in astonishing ways so that you're ready for anything and everything, more than just ready to do what needs to be done. As one psalmist puts it, He throws caution to the winds, giving to the needy in reckless abandon. His right-living, right-giving ways never run out, never wear out. This most generous God who gives seed to the farmer that becomes bread for your meals is more than extravagant with you. He gives you something you can then give away, which grows into full-formed lives, robust in God, wealthy in every way, so that you can be generous in every way, producing with us great praise to God. Carrying out this social relief work involves far more than helping meet the bare needs of poor Christians. It also produces abundant and bountiful thanksgivings to God. This relief offering is a prod to live at your very best, showing your gratitude to God by being openly obedient to the plain meaning of the Message of Christ. You show your gratitude through your generous offerings to your needy brothers and sisters, and really toward everyone. Meanwhile, moved by the extravagance of God in your lives, they'll respond by praying for you in passionate intercession for whatever you need. Thank God for this gift, his gift. No language can praise it enough!

(2 Corinthians 9:6–15 MSG)

Giving offerings is one of the most powerful ways we can worship God. We need always to be on the lookout for opportunities to give offerings. If I want to live a life that downloads heaven, I have to understand that it truly is more blessed to give than to receive. My life has to become an offering. Jesus wants us to become drink offerings. It's not just what I bring to the offering plate; it's also my very life that is an offering.

There was a man named Cornelius who lived in Caesarea, captain of the Italian Guard stationed there. He was a good man. He had led

everyone in his house to live worshipfully before God, was always help-
ing people in need, and had the habit of prayer. (Acts 10:1–2 MSG)

Cornelius exemplified what it means to lead others in a lifestyle of worship and giving. His lifestyle was ultimately responsible for the heavenly encounters that ushered his entire household into the kingdom of God. If you want to usher your family and friends into the kingdom of God, live a lifestyle of worship and giving.

A = Appraisal

Doxa is a Greek word for worship referring to "an opinion or estimate concerning someone that results in praise, honor, glory, splendor, brightness, excellence, preeminence, dignity, grace and majesty." *Doxa* worship is an appraisal of God.

How much do you estimate God to be worth? What is your estimation of Him and His glory? Not long ago, we had an auto accident, and an insurance appraiser was sent to evaluate the damage to our car. After the inspection, the company sent us a check to pay for the necessary repairs. They first had to estimate and appraise the value of the damage. When I buy a house, an appraisal of the house gives me the ability to present the bank with information that will result in a loan to purchase the house. The appraisal identifies what I should spend for it. I do not want to pay more than the appraised value. If I'm smart, I will try to get the seller to reduce the price to an amount less than the appraisal value.

There are people whose appraisal of God is way too low. Their *doxa* of God is too low. We have to get to a place where our appraisal of God considers Him praise-worthy. Our appraisal of God should be so high that we are willing to bow down, that we are willing to dance and praise. We need to give Him the worship that He is due.

You will get to a place with God where He is everything to you and you are nothing without Him. Bow before Him. If you praise God as if you are doing Him a favor, or if it is more about you than it is about Him, then you will miss out on your upload. Your worship needs to be a lavish offering! Your heart cannot remain far from Him. It cannot pay Him lip service. You can't be praising Him in earnest and remain far from Him. When you have moved to a place of genuine expression, there is a difference in your praise. You should put your heart, emotions, and affection into your words. This is why you should come to church. If your heart remains back at the restaurant, if your heart is on your stack of bills, or if your heart is on the ball game, it isn't on God.

Doesn't it irritate you when you are doing something on your computer and you lose your wireless signal? When that happens, you lose whatever it was you were doing. When the same thing happens to your praise of God, don't you think that disappoints God, as well? You are uploading praise when, all of a sudden, you're distracted and you disconnect. That's how it seems to God. We start to worship Him, but then we get a text. We're worshipping Him, but then the phone rings. We're worshipping Him, but then we need to look at our phone or iPad. When we get distracted in our worship, it results in slow or failed downloads from heaven. Instead of being distracted worshippers, we need to be Davidic worshippers! Then we will experience high-speed downloads of heaven's glory into our lives.

Your appraisal of God is a reverse appraisal, in that it actually appraises you! If my appraisal of God is low, then my appraisal of His house is low. Then, my appraisal of God becomes a reverse appraisal of my own life. If I don't value Him, I won't value myself. If I don't put the right value on my covenant with God, I won't value my own marriage. My appraisal of God flows into every relationship I have.

I want my *doxa* of God to be off the charts. I want to upload an appraisal of God, the best appraisal I can offer. In fact, if I praise Him to the best of my ability, it still would not be enough. So, I have to give Him the best that I have. This becomes my sacrifice of praise. We can get a glimpse of what heaven is like through John's eyes in the following passage:

After these things I looked, and behold, a door standing open in heaven. And the first voice which I heard was like a trumpet speaking with me, saying, "Come up here, and I will show you things which must take place after this." Immediately I was in the Spirit; and behold, a throne set in heaven, and One sat on the throne. And He who sat there was like a jasper and a sardius stone in appearance; and there was a rainbow around the throne, in appearance like an emerald. Around the throne were twenty-four thrones, and on the thrones I saw twenty-four elders sitting, clothed in white robes; and they had crowns of gold on their heads. And from the throne proceeded lightnings, thunderings, and voices. Seven lamps of fire were burning before the throne, which are the seven Spirits of God. Before the throne there was a sea of glass, like crystal. And in the midst of the throne, and around the throne, were four living creatures full of eyes in front and in back. The first living creature was like a lion, the second living creature like a calf, the third living creature had a face like a man, and the fourth living creature was like a flying eagle. The four living creatures, each having six wings, were full of eyes around and within. And they do not rest day or night, saying: "Holy, holy, holy, Lord God Almighty, who was and is and is to come!" Whenever the living creatures give glory and honor and thanks to Him who sits on the throne, who lives forever and ever, the twenty-four elders fall down before Him who sits on the throne and worship Him who lives forever and ever, and cast their crowns before the throne, saying: "You are worthy, O Lord, to receive glory and honor and power; for You created all things, and by Your will they exist and were created."

(Revelation 4:1–11)

As I stated before, I encountered the Lord as a sixteen-year-old at a church in Wisconsin. He opened up heaven, and I hit my knees. I heard heaven; I heard worship like I had never heard before. I heard the sounds of His presence. He said, "Worship Me! It is the closest place on earth to Me. Teach My people to worship Me!" From that place of worship, from that place of intimacy, I have tried to live my life. This passage gives us a glimpse of that, as He begins to tell us that even as passionate worship happens around the throne, we also need to see that here on the earth.

Thou art worthy, O Lord, to receive glory and honour and power: for thou hast created all things, and for thy pleasure they are and were created.   (Revelation 4:11 KJV)

Remember this statement: *"For thy pleasure they are and were created."* You were created to upload prophetic praise and worship and to download heaven on earth. When you realize that you were created for God's pleasure, you will experience what I call a "change of address." You will move from the slow lanes of "poverty circle" to the fast lanes of I-320, or E-320—aka Ephesians 3:20!

Now to Him Who, by (in consequence of) the [action of His] power that is at work within us, is able to [carry out His purpose and] do superabundantly, far over and above all that we [dare] ask or think [infinitely beyond our highest prayers, desires, thoughts, hopes, or dreams]—to Him be glory in the church and in Christ Jesus throughout all generations forever and ever. Amen (so be it).   (Ephesians 3:20–21 AMP)

The thief comes only in order to steal and kill and destroy. I came that they may have and enjoy life, and have it in abundance (to the full, till it overflows).   (John 10:10 AMP)

A thief is only there to steal and kill and destroy. I came so they can have real and eternal life, more and better life than they ever dreamed of.   (John 10:10 MSG)

The overflowing life is such a download that glory just squishes out of your shoes wherever you walk. You will be permeated with His presence. Why? Because you sent the evaporation, or prophetic praise, up to heaven, and then it came back down in the form of rain. You'll be able to say to your neighbors and coworkers, "What do you need? Is it healing? Get close to me, because I have been spending time with the Healer! You need breakthrough in your finances? Spend time with me, because I have been spending time with the God who owns it all. You need favor? I have been rubbing shoulders with the King of Kings; I have been laying my head on His chest and loving Him. I just happen to know Someone who can do something for you! It doesn't come from here on earth; it comes from spending time with Him."

> Seek first the kingdom of God and His righteousness, and all these things shall be added to you.   (Matthew 6:33)

D = Demonstration

To demonstrate something is to clearly prove its existence by offering evidence. It is to show or express something by your actions.

For example, God demonstrated His love for us, His children, by sending His Son Jesus to die for our sins.

> God went for the jugular when he sent his own Son. He didn't deal with the problem as something remote and unimportant. In his Son, Jesus, he personally took on the human condition, entered the disordered mess of struggling humanity in order to set it right once and for all. The law code, weakened as it always was by fractured human nature, could never have done that. The law always ended up being used as a Band-Aid on sin instead of a deep healing of it. And now what the law code asked for but we couldn't deliver is accomplished as we, instead of redoubling our own efforts, simply embrace what the Spirit is doing in us. Those who think they can do it on their own end up obsessed with measuring their own moral muscle but never get around to exercising it in real life. Those who trust God's action in them find that God's Spirit is in them—living and breathing God! Obsession with self in these matters is a dead end; attention to God leads us out into the open, into a spacious, free life. Focusing on the self is the opposite of focusing on God. Anyone completely absorbed in self ignores God, ends up thinking more about self than God. That person ignores who God is and what he is doing. And God isn't pleased at being ignored. But if God himself has taken up residence

in your life, you can hardly be thinking more of yourself than of him. Anyone, of course, who has not welcomed this invisible but clearly present God, the Spirit of Christ, won't know what we're talking about. But for you who welcome him, in whom he dwells—even though you still experience all the limitations of sin—you yourself experience life on God's terms. It stands to reason, doesn't it, that if the alive-and-present God who raised Jesus from the dead moves into your life, he'll do the same thing in you that he did in Jesus, bringing you alive to himself? When God lives and breathes in you (and he does, as surely as he did in Jesus), you are delivered from that dead life. With his Spirit living in you, your body will be as alive as Christ's!...This resurrection life you received from God is not a timid, grave-tending life. It's adventurously expectant, greeting God with a childlike "What's next, Papa?" God's Spirit touches our spirits and confirms who we really are. We know who he is, and we know who we are: Father and children. And we know we are going to get what's coming to us—an unbelievable inheritance! We go through exactly what Christ goes through. If we go through the hard times with him, then we're certainly going to go through the good times with him!   (Romans 8:3–11, 15–17 MSG)

First Kings 4:29–34 is such an amazing display of God's glory and power. *"God gave Solomon wisdom..."* (1 Kings 4:29 MSG). Pause for a minute! What has God told us about wisdom?

If any of you lacks wisdom, let him ask of God, who gives to all liberally and without reproach, and it will be given to him.   (James 1:5)

This verse is one of my daily prayers: "God, I need more wisdom!" Let's continue in 1 Kings 4:

God gave Solomon wisdom—the deepest of understanding and the largest of hearts. There was nothing beyond him, nothing he couldn't handle.   (1 Kings 4:29 MSG)

God, I want to be like that!

Solomon's wisdom outclassed the vaunted wisdom of wise men of the East, outshone the famous wisdom of Egypt. He was wiser than anyone—wiser than Ethan the Ezrahite, wiser than Heman, wiser than Calcol and Darda the sons of Mahol. He became famous among all the surrounding nations. He created 3,000 proverbs; his songs added up to 1,005. He knew all about plants, from the huge cedar that grows in Lebanon to the tiny hyssop that grows in the cracks of a wall. He understood everything about animals and birds, reptiles and fish. Sent by kings from all over the earth who had heard of his reputation, people came from far and near to listen to the wisdom of Solomon.

(1 Kings 4:30–34 MSG)

Talk about a demonstration! How many of you want more wisdom? Wisdom is a demonstration of God's glory. But we must remember that it goes beyond the wisdom of men. It's important that we demonstrate the kingdom through supernatural displays of God's power. In order to do so, we must live out of the Spirit and not out of our own heads. We cannot lean on our own understanding and know-how. (See Proverbs 3:5–6.) This is a must if we're going to raise up disciples with strong faith in God's power instead of in their own wisdom.

*And my speech and my preaching were not with persuasive words of human wisdom, but in **demonstration** of the Spirit and of power, that your faith should not be in the wisdom of men but in the power of God.* (1 Corinthians 2:4–5)

*God's Way is not a matter of mere talk; it's an **empowered life**.*
(1 Corinthians 4:20 MSG)

2

BECOMING A GOVERNOR OF PRAISE

D id you know that praising and worshipping God is one of the most powerful things you can do? So many churches consider praise and worship to only be part of the preliminaries in a service, or, at best, something to prepare the people to hear the Word of God. When most Christians think of making a difference in their world, they immediately think of things like missions, outreach, prayer, or acts of service. Although these ministries are important and needed in the body of Christ, what is really needed to shake the nations and change lives in this day and hour is for God's people to become what I call "governors of praise."

Let's take a look at a Bible verse that explains this concept:

In that day I will make the governors of Judah like a firepan in the woodpile, and like a fiery torch in the sheaves; they shall devour all the surrounding peoples on the right hand and on the left, but Jerusalem shall be inhabited again in her own place—Jerusalem.

(Zechariah 12:6)

In the very first phrase of this verse, the Lord mentions the *"governors of Judah."* Judah was one of the twelve tribes of Israel, but the prophecies that related to these tribes are applicable to us as the church today—as a kind of "new Israel." The name *Judah* actually means "praise."[1] So, this verse is describing what will happen when the governors of Judah, the governors of praise, come forth and begin to accomplish the work that God has destined for them.

God wants you, me, and all of the members of His church today to become "governors of praise." He says, *"In that day"*—I believe that day is now—"*I will make the governors of Judah* [the governors of praise] *like a firepan in the woodpile, and like a fiery torch in the sheaves.*" The word *"torch"* can also refer to lightning. Did you know that there is lightning around the throne of God? (See, for example, Revelation 4:5.) A lightning bolt is a powerful release of energy. Things like that happen around God's throne! Destinies are released, promises are fulfilled, and territories are taken for God's kingdom. When God's governors of praise begin to rise up, lightning begins to strike in the heavenlies! Things begin to shift in atmospheres so that people can be set free.

Zechariah 12:6 continues, *"They shall devour all the surrounding peoples on the right hand and on the left...."* The word *"peoples"* in this instance means "nations."[2] Do you want to see the nations come and submit themselves to the glory of God? The Word says that the knowledge of the glory of the Lord will cover the earth as the waters cover the sea. (See Habakkuk 2:14.) But that will not happen until God's governors of praise rise up and begin to inhabit Jerusalem through the power of the Spirit of God.

The Bible says that we are seated together with Christ in heavenly places.

> *But God, who is rich in mercy, because of His great love with which He loved us, even when we were dead in trespasses, made us alive together with Christ (by grace you have been saved), and raised us*

---

1. *Strong's Concordance* #H3063.
2. *Strong's Concordance* #H5971.

up together, and made us sit together in the heavenly places in Christ Jesus. (Ephesians 2:4–6)

This means that we must take on a governing role in our praise. Our praise is not supposed to just be words mouthed from a defeated position here on the earth. No! Our praise is supposed to take place from a position of victory, from up in the heavens, sitting in those seats from which we look down on the enemy. We don't look at the enemy here on earth in order to prophesy against something that's over us, but we take our seats as judges and as governors in the heavens. We speak against those forces of darkness that are beneath our feet. The Bible says that God has put all things beneath the feet of Jesus. (See 1 Corinthians 15:25, 27; Ephesians 1:22; Hebrews 2:8.) But the Word also says, *"The God of peace will crush satan under your feet shortly"* (Romans 16:20). Are you ready to see satan crushed beneath your feet? I don't know if the shoes you wear are size 11, size 12, or even size 4. It doesn't matter! When you become a governor of praise, God begins to crush satan under your feet, and you begin to walk in victory!

Shut the Devil Up!

Many Christians share this common misunderstanding about praise: "Praising God builds me up and helps to strengthen my spirit." While that is certainly true, that is not all praise and worship does.

Let's take a look at one verse that will give us a greater understanding of what exactly takes place when we praise and worship God.

Out of the mouth of babes and nursing infants You have ordained strength ["praise" NIV], *because of Your enemies, that You may silence the enemy and the avenger.* (Psalm 8:2)

When Jesus quoted this passage, He said, *"Out of the mouth of babes and nursing infants You have perfected praise"* (Matthew 21:16). So, we see that *strength* and *praise* are synonymous. When you praise God, you receive strength. If you need strength, you need to praise God! The Bible says that the joy of the Lord is your strength, and you receive joy in the presence of the Lord. (See Nehemiah 8:10.) In His presence there is fullness of joy and life forevermore. (See Psalm 16:11.) God inhabits the praises of His people. (See Psalm 22:3 KJV.) So, if you want more joy in your life, you just need more of God's presence. Once you receive His presence, you receive joy and strength for the battles you face.

The *New International Version* renders Matthew 21:16 as follows: *"From the lips of children and infants you have ordained praise."* When we look at this in its original context, Psalm 8:2, we might ask the question, "God has ordained praise for what reason?" The answer is clear: Because of the enemies of the Lord.

This directly contradicts the idea that praise is only for us—or even for God's benefit. But God has made it clear: He has ordained praise so that we might overcome the enemies of God; that we might still the enemy and the avenger. In other words, God has ordained praise so that we might shut the devil up! Do you want to shut the devil up and keep his voice out of your life? The way to do that is through the praise and worship of God!

There is governmental praise. This is a role you can take in the heavenlies. You can take your seat with Christ in the spiritual realm and begin to speak forth the praises of God. This suggests that there is an importance attached to the words that you speak. Praising God does not include saying, "Oh Lord, please, I beg of You…" or "Oh God, I don't know if You are going to fulfill Your promises…" or "I just don't know if it's Your will…." No! Praise knows the will of the Father, and it speaks forth that will into the earth. When true praise goes forth, it silences the enemy!

When you are truly praising and worshipping the living God, there will be no room for fear in your life. You won't have any fear of the devil or of what he might do to you, because you will know that greater is He who is within you than he that is in the world. (See 1 John 4:4.) You will know beyond a shadow of a doubt that all of God's plans for you are for good, and not evil, and that when you are governing your life and the territory around you with praise, His will and His good plans will come to pass!

Governors of Praise Are Too Hot to Handle

Do you want to be too hot for the devil to handle? Do you want to be too bold for him to hold? Let's look again at our key passage to see how we can keep the enemy from gaining any kind of foothold in our lives—through praise:

> *In that day I will make the **governors of Judah** like a firepan in the woodpile, and like a fiery torch in the sheaves; they shall devour all the surrounding peoples on the right hand and on the left, but Jerusalem shall be inhabited again in her own place—Jerusalem.*
>
> (Zechariah 12:6)

The word for *"firepan"* here can also be translated as "hearth."[3] In Old Testament times, a hearth was a chafing dish for coals or a cauldron used for cooking. God says that He will make us like "hearths of fire"; in other words, He will make us into places that "cook things up" for His kingdom. He wants us to turn up the heat in the kitchen and make it so hot that the devil can't stand to be there anymore!

Unfortunately, many churches today that are so lukewarm, and their praise and worship so weak, that the devil has taken up residence there. Did you know that you can allow the praise and worship in your church to become so "user-friendly" that it becomes unfriendly to God? Worship is not about us; it's all about Him, and what He *can* and *will* do through us when we make Him and His authority our number one priority. We need to become God-friendly and Holy Spirit-sensitive instead of user-friendly and seeker-sensitive. Instead of being concerned with how many people we can get into the building, we need to be focused on how much of *God* we can attract through our worship. After all, it's when He is truly lifted up that all will be drawn to Him!

The difference can be seen when you enter a house of worship where governors of praise are operating. Devils cannot abide in that place! In

---

3. *Strong's Concordance* #H3595.

that place, the people cry out, "Let God arise and let His enemies be scattered!" (See Psalm 68:1.) When you are in a church where God is arising in the midst of the people, His enemies scatter. They can't dwell in His presence. It is so wonderful to be in a church service where the presence of God is welcomed. Sickness and disease can't stay in that meeting. When someone with cancer or another type of disease enters, the disease can't stay, because the presence of God overwhelms the adversary.

That's what occurs when you *turn up the heat*! God wants us to be on fire for Him, because when we are, miracles, signs, and wonders take place. The trouble comes about when we are lukewarm—neither hot nor cold. In Revelation 3, Jesus said that if we are lukewarm, He will spew us out of His mouth. (See Revelation 3:16 KJV.) Many churches today are lukewarm. Jesus wants us to be hot. We must decide whether we're in or out. Are you in it to win it? Or are you just trying to survive until tomorrow, when you'll get up and do the same thing all over again?

Another meaning of the Hebrew word for "*firepan*" is "platform, stage." God was saying that He would make the governors of Judah—the governors of praise—to be like a platform or stage, from which He would make proclamations. God wants to make His announcements to the world through us—his governors of praise! When He releases those decrees and declarations from our pulpits, it will silence the enemy in our region. See, our praise is not just for the house of God, its origination, but it is to go out into the atmosphere and effect change on the nations of the world.

The word "*torch*" in Zechariah 12:6 also has a special meaning. It is derived from a Hebrew root word meaning "to shine."[4] God wants us to arise and shine among His people, today!

> *Arise, shine; for your light has come! And the glory of the* Lord *is risen upon you. For behold, the darkness shall cover the earth, and deep darkness the people; but the* Lord *will arise over you, and His glory will be seen upon you. The Gentiles shall come to your light, and kings to the brightness of your rising.* (Isaiah 60:1–3)

---

4. *Strong's Concordance* #H3940.

Our light has come, and the glory of the Lord has risen upon us. The Hebrew word for *"torch"* in Zechariah 12:6 also means a "lamp…burning." Are you ready to see something catch fire and begin to burn inside of you? Most of us, when we first were saved, felt as if we were overcome with passion and zeal. But, over time, unless we've been careful, that passion may have begun to die off. Can you remember the zeal for God you used to have? Do you recall when you just couldn't wait to get into the presence of God? You had to be at God's house. You had to be in prayer. You had to read the Bible. Today, God is looking for people who will return to the state of burning with passion for God, for His house, and for prayer.

Zechariah 12:6 tells us where the torch is to be lit: *"in the sheaves."* The Hebrew word for *"sheaves"* can also mean "a handful."[5] Do you want to see God's hands wrapped around you? When we have a handful—a grasp of God's purposes in His body, then the hand of God, or the fivefold ministries (see Ephesians 4:11), will begin to operate like never before, bringing change like lightning in the region.

A firepan in the hearth and a fiery torch in the sheaves—these are what God desires His governors of praise to become in the earth!

Your kingdom come. Your will be done on earth as it is in heaven.
(Matthew 6:10)

Just as it is in heaven, God is raising up burning ones who will release heaven on earth. You and I were born to burn! We are called to be people who burn fervently with a lovesick passion for our Savior!

I watched till thrones were put in place, and the Ancient of Days was seated; His garment was white as snow, and the hair of His head was like pure wool. His throne was a fiery flame, its wheels a burning fire; a fiery steam issued and came forth from before Him.
(Daniel 7:9–10)

Our God is a consuming fire (see Hebrews 12:29), and from His fiery throne issues a river of fire. As we spend time in His presence, we will

5. *Strong's Concordance* #H5995.

come forth in kingdom demonstration as burning ones who are "too hot to handle" and too bold to hold for the forces of darkness.

Governors of Praise Reap Promised Blessings

Genesis 49 lists the blessings and promises that were given to the sons of Jacob—the sons of Israel. Each son received certain prophetic blessings, but the tribe of Judah was special. Remember, the word *Judah* means "praise." When we begin to move into the calling of praise and worship that God has for us, we will begin to see these blessings of Judah manifest in our lives and in the life of God's church.

Judah, you are he whom your brothers shall praise; your hand shall be on the neck of your enemies; your father's children shall bow down before you. Judah is a lion's whelp; from the prey, my son, you have gone up. He bows down, he lies down as a lion; and as a lion, who shall rouse him? The scepter shall not depart from Judah, nor a lawgiver from between his feet, until Shiloh comes; and to Him shall be the obedience of the people. Binding his donkey to the vine, and his donkey's colt to the choice vine, he washed his garments in wine, and his clothes in the blood of grapes. His eyes are darker than wine, and his teeth whiter than milk. (Genesis 49:8–12)

God's Word is so good! He gives us such insight and strategy on how to defeat the enemy in our lives. The first thing the Lord tells us in this passage is that the hand of Judah, or the hand of praise, will be "on" the neck of our enemies. The King James Version actually says, "*Thy hand shall be in the neck of thine enemies*" (Genesis 49:8). Have you ever seen a Bruce Lee movie in which the hero spins around and goes straight for the jugular vein of his enemy? That's what our praise can do to the devil: it can strike him in the neck—the jugular; in his vocal cords, even. For some of us, it is crucial to cast down the lying words of the enemy.

When we begin to worship God with our own voices, that praise goes into the "neck" of our enemy and silences him. Again, that's why God said that He has ordained praise and strength—to shut the devil up. Praise paralyzes the vocal cords of darkness and causes your enemy to scatter in the mighty name of Jesus!

There are so many benefits of becoming a governor of praise. Judah's *"father's children"* bow down before him. Judah is a *"lion's whelp"*; the scepter will not depart from him. Where there are governors of praise, the scepter—the authority of the Lord—will not depart from that place. When God arises with a shout, all His enemies are scattered, and His purposes are realized in the earth.

It is important to understand something about the scepter of Judah, also called the scepter of praise. When the scepter of a king or queen is extended to a person, everything that person asks for—anything he or she desires—is granted. When the scepter was extended to her, Esther could enter the throne room and make her petitions known to her husband, King Xerxes. (See Esther 4:11; 5:2; 8:4.) Many of us want to see God answer our prayers, yet all we're doing is crying and pleading and begging Him to do something. But God tells us to rise up as governors of praise! He says, "Begin to make My name glorious, to make My praise glorious in the earth; and when you do, My scepter will stay with you, and everything you ask will be granted."

The Word says, *"The scepter shall not depart from Judah, nor a lawgiver from between his feet, until Shiloh comes; and to Him shall be the obedience of the people"* (Genesis 49:10). The King James Version says, *"And unto him shall the gathering of the people be."* Do you want to see the gathering of nations? Do you want to see the gathering of the heathen, the gathering of the lost who are coming to God? That will take place when there are governors of praise seated in heavenly places with Christ, making His praise glorious.

✗ The church today seems to value marketing programs. We have become "user-friendly," more focused on building a social club than advancing the kingdom of God. It is possible to have a "golden calf society" in church, where everybody shines each other's armor and looks pretty. In that case, we can all become navel-gazers who never actually accomplish anything for the kingdom. But when people rise up and begin to praise

God, religious folk begin to leave, devils begin to scream, and God's kingdom is established, His scepter is extended, and the lost truly begin to be gathered in!

Jesus said, *"And I, if I am lifted up from the earth, will draw all peoples to Myself"* (John 12:32). When we praise and worship Jesus Christ, the lost from all nations of the earth will be drawn to the Father. Jesus says to His church, in effect, "When I find some governors of praise, when I find some people who will sit with Me in heavenly places, when I find some people who will make My praise glorious, there will My scepter be. There will I rise and draw all men unto Me."

When my son, Hunter, was twelve years old, he did a project at his Christian school in which his teacher asked him to compare God to a magnet. That was an easy project! I found many Scriptures to help him—so many that he began to say, "Thanks, Dad—that's enough!" The truth is, the Bible is filled with references to the "magnetism" of God. God has said that when we draw near to Him, He will draw near to us. (See James 4:8.) When we begin to praise the Lord, when we begin to express our love for Jesus, and when we begin to glorify the Father, He will glorify us. He will glorify His house, the church, with His glory. When there's a people who will draw close to Him and will lift Him up, He says He will draw people to Himself. If you have a desire, a longing, to see lost people come to Jesus, then begin to praise Him, and watch how He begins to move to save people and deliver them!

Governors of Praise Prevail Through Persecution and Raise a Place of Praise

The true gospel is not a "user-friendly" gospel. Many people believe that after they come to Christ, all of their problems will be solved. Nothing could be further from the truth! The Bible tells of many believers who were persecuted for their faith. I like to say that when you accept Christ, you're going to catch hell—but you don't have to hold on to it!

I appreciate everything that the Word of Faith movement has done for the church. Certainly, there is a lot of truth in the idea that the words you speak in a given situation will help to shape the outcome of that situation. But when people somehow come up with the misguided notion that everything will be perfect if they just have enough faith to overcome, unfortunately, it shows that they have taken the teaching to an extreme. That doctrine is not taught in Scripture. Many of us want to know God in the power of His resurrection, but we forget that we must also participate in the fellowship of His sufferings. (See Philippians 3:10.) We believe that if we just had enough faith, then we wouldn't have to go through certain situations. I think the apostle Paul would have had to disagree!

Throughout the course of his ministry, Paul wrote two-thirds of the New Testament, established churches throughout the known world, and saw hundreds of people converted by his preaching. But he also faced imprisonment, stonings, shipwrecks, and snake bites! We all say we want to be like the apostle Paul—until it's time for the persecution. Paul was a man of faith and power, but he still ended up in jail.

Let's take a look at what happened in one instance of his imprisonment.

> Now it happened, as we went to prayer, that a certain slave girl possessed with a spirit of divination met us, who brought her masters much profit by fortune-telling. This girl followed Paul and us, and cried out, saying, "These men are the servants of the Most High God, who proclaim to us the way of salvation." And this she did for many days. But Paul, greatly annoyed, turned and said to the spirit, "I command you in the name of Jesus Christ to come out of her." And he came out that very hour. But when her masters saw that their hope of profit was gone, they seized Paul and Silas and dragged them into the marketplace to the authorities. (Acts 16:16–19)

In most cases, we would believe that casting a demon out of a person and setting her free would be a *good* thing. But, at this time, Paul was being persecuted for ministering the love and power of Jesus Christ.

And they brought them to the magistrates, and said, "These men, being Jews, exceedingly trouble our city; and they teach customs which are not lawful for us, being Romans, to receive or observe." Then the multitude rose up together against them; and the magistrates tore off their clothes and commanded them to be beaten with rods. And when they had laid many stripes on them, they threw them into prison, commanding the jailer to keep them securely. Having received such a charge, he put them into the inner prison and fastened their feet in the stocks. (Acts 16:20–24)

What would most of us do in a situation like this? What would you do? I think most of us would whine and complain—but not Paul and Silas.

But at midnight Paul and Silas were praying and singing hymns to God, and the prisoners were listening to them. Suddenly there was a great earthquake, so that the foundations of the prison were shaken; and immediately all the doors were opened and everyone's chains were loosed. And the keeper of the prison, awaking from sleep and seeing the prison doors open, supposing the prisoners had fled, drew his sword and was about to kill himself. But Paul called with a loud voice, saying, "Do yourself no harm, for we are all here." Then he called for a light, ran in, and fell down trembling before Paul and Silas. And he brought them out and said, "Sirs, what must I do to be saved?" So they said, "Believe on the Lord Jesus Christ, and you will be saved, you and your household." Then they spoke the word of the Lord to him and to all who were in his house. And he took them the same hour of the night and washed their stripes. And immediately he and all his family were baptized. Now when he had brought them into his house, he set food before them; and he rejoiced, having believed in God with all his household. (Acts 16:25–34)

Historians tell us that the sewers of the day ran directly through the Roman jails. Paul and Silas were very likely being held in the lower parts of the dungeon, where the stench of sewage was running by their feet, perhaps even over their feet. They were in shackles. They were in bondage.

Historians have also said that, many times, Roman jailers would leave prisoners in chains long after they were dead, so it is feasible that Paul and Silas may have been strapped in chains with corpses on either side of them.

Can you imagine? Most people in the church today would have given up at that point. In fact, many of us will give up if we get an unexpected bill in the mail or if somebody talks negatively about us—we call *that* persecution. Persecution in the Bible was when Christians were boiled in hot water and tar, or when the flesh of believers was pulled from their bones.

But the apostles Paul and Silas, even in the midst of their terrible situation, said, "Let's sing and praise God!" The Bible says that when they prayed and sang praises to God, the prison began to shake. Glory to God! Do you want to see things start to shake around you? Begin to praise the Lord in your situation and then watch things begin to move!

You might be familiar with "Jailhouse Rock," a song made famous by Elvis Presley. But, let me tell you, Elvis wasn't the original writer of that song! Paul and Silas wrote the original "Jailhouse Rock." That song was written when Paul and Silas began to praise God in the midnight hour. The place began to shake, and there was a jailhouse rock. The doors swung open, and the Bible says that not only Paul and Silas but *everyone* in the prison was set free. The jailer—the one who had been persecuting them—was even led to the Lord, along with his entire family. (See Acts 16:26–33.)

Remember Genesis 49:10, where the Lord said, in effect, "I'm going to make you a hearth of fire; I'm going to cause all nations to come to you"? There will be a gathering of the people where there's praise.

When you begin to praise God, prison doors open. If you go to your job and you whine and cry about how lost everyone is, nothing is going to happen. But if you go to your job a few minutes early and praise God over that place, anoint that place with prayer, and spend your lunch breaks praying, I guarantee that you'll start shifting the heavens over that place, all because you're taking your seat—a rightful seat in the heavenly places.

Prison doors open when we follow David's model of praise. Consider Amos 9:11:

> *On that day I will raise up the tabernacle of David, which has fallen down, and repair its damages; I will raise up its ruins, and rebuild it as in the days of old.*

David went beyond his dispensation into another dispensation, recognizing that the sacrifice of praise to God was more excellent than the sacrifice of goats and lambs. (See, for example, Jeremiah 33:11.) He would offer the sacrifice of praise. And because of this praise that took place, David conquered all of the enemies that Joshua had failed to defeat. Why? Because he established the tabernacle of David, brought in the ark of the covenant, and said, "We're going to minister to God continuously in this temple—twenty-four-seven, three hundred sixty-five days a year!" Some three thousand musicians were appointed and paid to stay at the house of God, constantly praising Him. From that point on, every enemy and adversary of God was put under David's feet.

Do you want to see all of your enemies put beneath your feet? Do what David did. David established the place of praise, to worship God continually. But now, take a look at the next verse in Amos, which explains the purpose of the raising of the tabernacle:

> *"That they may possess the remnant of Edom, and all the Gentiles who are called by My name," says the* LORD *who does this thing.*
> (Amos 9:12)

Notice those words: *"that they may possess."* Are you a possessor? Do you have in your possession the promises of the Lord?

> *"Behold, the days are coming," says the* LORD, *"when the plowman shall overtake the reaper, and the treader of grapes him who sows seed; the mountains shall drip with sweet wine, and all the hills shall flow with it."*
> (Amos 9:13)

When David's fallen tent is restored, when the praises of God are raised once again, the people will rise up as governors of praise and establish God's throne. The scepter of the Lord will be extended over regions and over territories, so that the heathen will come to know the God of the universe. Do you want to see the new wine of God in the house? Do you want to see the praise of the Lord make a difference in the lives of your loved ones, your community, your nation, and the world? Do you want to possess the land and claim the promises that God has for you? Praise will put you into that land and keep you there!

This isn't just an Old Testament promise. Take a look at Acts 15:16–18:

> *"After this I will return and will rebuild the tabernacle of David, which has fallen down; I will rebuild its ruins, and I will set it up; so that the rest of mankind may seek the* Lord, *even all the Gentiles who are called by My name, says the* Lord *who does all these things." Known to God from eternity are all His works.*

The tabernacle of David has fallen down, but God has promised to restore it and set it up. God is saying in this hour, "I need some governors of praise. I need some people who will arise and build Me a tabernacle of worship." Why? So people will seek the Lord! From the beginning of the world, my friend, God planned for there to be a Davidic company—governors of Judah, governors of praise—who would raise up the tabernacle of David so that the lost would be able to come to the saving knowledge of Jesus. These "pre-believers" are going to come to know our God! Do you have any unsaved loved ones? God's promise is for you. There are pre-believers in your life who are going to come to know God because you have risen up as a governor of praise!

3

THREE PHASES OF PRAISE

The Lord has given this word to me: there are three phases of praise through which His people must pass. This is not some rhyme I came up with on my own. I was praying in my prayer language one day, and these words came up out of my spirit. I know they are from the living God and that they are a powerful word to help His people become the governors of praise He has called them to be.

Phase One: Penetrate

When you begin to move into praise, you have to penetrate through the forces of darkness with your praise, into the heavenlies, where you can take your rightful place in the kingdom of God.

Phase Two: Saturate

In the saturation phase, once you have penetrated into the Holy of Holies, you are saturated with His presence.

Phase Three: Permeate

In the third phase of praise, you become so saturated, so filled with the Spirit, that you permeate the earth with God's presence.

Penetrating, Saturating, and Permeating

God wants you to rise up to His throne in praise; that's the only way you will be able to accomplish what He wants to do through you. You must enter into His gates with thanksgiving and into His courts with praise. (See Psalm 100:4.) The only way you can enter God's presence is if you do so in praise. When you enter His courts with praise, He begins to saturate you with His glory. And then He sends you back down to the earth to rain on the dry land, permeating the world with His presence.

So many people in the church today have been praying for rain. "Oh, God," they pray, "send Your rain!" But those who pray that prayer may not be aware of the fact that they were actually praying for themselves. *We are the rain that God wants to shower down upon a dry and thirsty land!*

God's Word is so powerful, and it tells us what the rain—you and I— can accomplish for His kingdom:

> *"For My thoughts are not your thoughts, nor are your ways My ways," says the LORD. "For as the heavens are higher than the earth, so are My ways higher than your ways, and My thoughts than your thoughts. For as the rain comes down, and the snow from heaven, and do not return there, but water the earth, and make it bring forth and bud, that it may give seed to the sower and bread to the eater, so shall My word be that goes forth from My mouth; it shall not return to Me void, but it shall accomplish what I please, and it shall prosper in the thing for which I sent it."* (Isaiah 55:8–11)

God's ways are higher than our ways; His thoughts are greater than our thoughts! But as the rain comes down, God's Word goes forth and accomplishes His purposes in the earth. It gives seed to the sower and bread to the eater. Through these verses, God is showing us how true praise is formed. It is formed in the earth and released in the earth, when we come into the place of praise.

Have you ever wondered how rain actually forms? As I explained briefly in chapter 1, there is barometric pressure in the earth that causes gravitation, a pulling, and the heavens begin to pull up water from the earth—from oceans, lakes, rivers, and other bodies of water. When this pressure, by which water is drawn up into the heavens, gets to the right point, all the water that has been pulled up is released back to the earth. Therefore, in order for there to be rain on the earth, there must first be water already present on the earth, so that it can be pulled up and released back down.

Can you see the parallel in the spiritual realm? God is saying, in effect, "I am searching the earth for people who have My Word in their mouths—those who know how to speak forth praise so that I can pull it up into heaven and release it like rain back down to earth!"

Producing "Proceeding Praise"

In Matthew 4, Jesus spoke forth the Word of God when He was facing temptation from the enemy, and in the process, He gave us an example of the power of what I call "proceeding praise":

> *Then Jesus was led up by the Spirit into the wilderness to be tempted by the devil. And when He had fasted forty days and forty nights, afterward He was hungry. Now when the tempter came to Him, he said, "If You are the Son of God, command that these stones become bread." But He answered and said, "It is written, 'Man shall not live by bread alone, but by every word that proceeds from the mouth of God.'"* (Matthew 4:1–4)

Jesus successfully dealt with the enemy by saying these words: "*It is written....*" Then He quoted the Scripture: "*Man shall not live by bread alone, but by every word that proceeds from the mouth of God.*" This is the proceeding Word of God—the proceeding praise that will move mountains, defeat the enemy, and usher in the kingdom of God on the earth.

When true governors of praise begin to rise up and take their place in the church, God's scepter is extended, and His kingdom is established. God begins to feed off of the Word—His own Word—which is the proceeding Word that is coming forth from the bellies of His governors of praise. As the Word says, *"He that believeth on me, as the scripture hath said, out of his belly shall flow rivers of living water"* (John 7:38 KJV). God begins to pull from the rivers of living water within us and release them to His throne. The book of Revelation states that there is a river that flows from God's throne, but it flows from us to Him and then back to us, just like the natural rain that we experience upon the earth.

What goes up must come down. If nothing goes up, nothing comes back down. If your mouth is shut, or if all you're sending out into the spiritual environment is murmuring and complaining, then that's all you will get back from the heavens. But when you send praise up to God's throne in the heavens, that praise is going to come back down and bless your life. It will go up into the spiritual atmosphere like condensation, but when it comes back down, it will drench you in an outpouring of blessing! When you send forth proceeding praise, it's the proceeding Word of God—and it will not return void. *"Man shall not live by bread alone, but by every word that proceeds out of the mouth of God."*

You'll never proceed into your destiny until there's a proceeding Word that advances before you. But when there's a proceeding Word, the entrance of His Word into your life, it will go forth and give you entrance into your destiny—all the wonderful, amazing things that God has for you.

Many people today are looking for their destiny. They're looking for breakthrough, but they're not willing to take their seat in heavenly places as governors of praise. It is only once we have done so that we will begin to penetrate into the heavenlies. Then God will saturate us with His glory, and we'll begin to permeate with His presence. Once we have reached the phase of permeation, the place that once was dry will begin to receive the rain from our lives. The R-A-I-N will cause us to R-E-I-G-N in the earth. We become His rain, and we will become His reign. We will begin to reign and to rule in the earth!

4

ARISE AND BUILD

But one of the elders said to me, "Do not weep. Behold, the Lion of the tribe of Judah, the Root of David, has prevailed to open the scroll and to loose its seven seals." (Revelation 5:5)

When you rise up to praise God, it has ramifications not just for you but also for future generations. Do you want to see your children blessed? Praise God. Do you want to see your grandchildren blessed? Praise God. Don't just sit back and refuse to participate when you go to church. When you enter into the house of God—and even when you're just in your living room, your car, or anywhere else—be militant with your praise! Lift up your hands, clap, and shout unto God with a voice of triumph. It's not about your own nature anymore. It's about the nature of the King of *"the Lion of the tribe of Judah"* who lives inside of you.

You don't have authority over your life anymore. You've been bought with a price. You've been purchased with the shed blood of Jesus Christ.

So, start acting like He has control over your life. Allow the Word of God to "brainwash" you—to renew your mind and change your thinking. The Word is better than a bar of soap for washing your mind. When you begin to speak it from your mouth, it will wash your thoughts and attitudes until, eventually, you'll find yourself acting like Christ, not like yourself. When you get enough of the Word in you, you'll start changing. When you come to church, your attitude won't be, "I have to praise God today"; it will be, "I have the high privilege and honor of praising God today!" When you get up in the morning, you'll recognize that you don't *have* to seek God early in the morning—you *get* to seek God before the cares and problems of the day begin.

When you engage in prophetic praise, there will be an intensity, a passion, and a fervency that will emerge in your relationship with the Father. The Word says, "*The effective, fervent prayer of a righteous man avails much*" (James 5:16). The word "*fervent*" in that verse conveys something that is able to put out energy. Think of it like the boiling point for a pot of water. People who engage in prophetic praise put out power until they reach a boiling point in their life. They're always hot—on fire for the things of God! They are too hot to handle and too bold for the devil to hold.

Too many Christians spend their lives being lukewarm. Remember, Jesus said, "*Because you are lukewarm, and neither cold nor hot, I will vomit you out of My mouth*" (Revelation 3:16). He'd rather you be either hot or cold. But to enter into prophetic praise on the earth today, we must be on fire for Him!

This isn't about you; it's about a harvest. Prophetic praisers draw the lost people of the world to the Lord. Those who don't know Jesus will be drawn to the brightness of our rising and the praise of God on our lips and in our lives. It is your destiny and your legacy to praise God prophetically. God preordained your life and set it up so you would be right where you are at this specific time in history.

There are several prophetic praisers depicted in Scripture, all of whom should be a pattern for your own life and destiny. In this chapter, we will focus on the prophetic praiser named Nehemiah.

*These lived in the days of Joiakim the son of Jeshua, the son of Jozadak,
and in the days of Nehemiah the governor, and of Ezra the priest, the
scribe.* (Nehemiah 12:26)

Nehemiah was a governor—a person appointed to rule over regions
and territories, just as we are called to do in our own generation. Jesus is
called the King of Kings. Which "kings" is He the "King" of? The Word
does not refer to an individual king who rules politically over nations. No,
this is referring to believers. We are kings and priests unto our God, the
King of Kings.

Nehemiah 2 paints a picture that will help us better understand the
life of Nehemiah.

*Then I said to them, "You see the distress that we are in, how Jerusalem
lies waste, and its gates are burned with fire. Come and let us build the
wall of Jerusalem, that we may no longer be a reproach." And I told
them of the hand of my God which had been good upon me, and also
of the king's words that he had spoken to me.* (Nehemiah 2:17–18)

In our day, we could replace the word *"Jerusalem"* with whatever town
or city we live in. Without the gates of praise being built up in our cities
and nation, we will become *"a reproach."* Prophetic praisers are builders
who inspire others to build, as well.

*So they said, "Let us rise up and build." Then they set their hands to
this good work.* (Nehemiah 2:18)

Child of God, you have to strengthen your hands for this good work.
What is the work that God has called *you* to do? What is your destiny in
Him? Strengthen your hands and prepare for it. Whatever He calls you
to do will be a good work, and you will be able to accomplish it when you
release His power and blessing into your life through praise.

*But when Sanballat the Horonite, Tobiah the Ammonite official,
and Geshem the Arab heard of it, they laughed at us and despised*

us, and said, "What is this thing that you are doing? Will you rebel against the king?" So I answered them, and said to them, "The God of heaven Himself will prosper us; therefore we His servants will arise and build." (Nehemiah 2:19–20)

It's inevitable that you will face opposition, just as Nehemiah did. But be encouraged—God will prosper you, and you will *"arise and build"*!

Ascend and Exercise Your Authority

Did you know that prophetic praisers proceed over legal matters in the heavenly realms? When you praise the Lord and take your seat of legal authority, you can bring the destiny of God to pass in your life.

Take a look at what the apostle Paul said in Ephesians 2:

But God, who is rich in mercy, because of His great love with which He loved us, even when we were dead in trespasses, made us alive together with Christ (by grace you have been saved), and raised us up together, and made us sit together in the heavenly places in Christ Jesus.... (Ephesians 2:4–6)

You have been granted a heavenly seat of authority. God wants you to proceed; He wants you to rule from this seat.

Praise causes you to possess the land. It's important for you to understand that if you're not praising, you're not possessing. You cease to possess when you cease to praise. The book of Judges helps us to understand this principle:

And the LORD said, "Judah shall go up. Indeed I have delivered the land into his hand." (Judges 1:2)

Praise will cause you to ascend. Praise will cause you to go up into greater things in the Lord! God says that He has delivered the land into the hand of Judah—the hand of praise. The land is delivered to a people of praise. Do you want to see your city and your nation come into the hands of the people of God? Praise will possess the land.

> So Judah said to Simeon his brother, "Come up with me to my allotted territory, that we may fight against the Canaanites; and I will likewise go with you to your allotted territory." And Simeon went with him.
> (Judges 1:3)

The name *Simeon* means "to hear, or one who hears."[6] Praise says to the hearers, "Come with me!" The Bible says, "*Simeon went with him.*" The hearers go with the praisers. The Bible tells us that faith comes by hearing, and hearing by the Word of the Lord. (See Romans 10:17.) When we begin to lift our praise to God, it releases a sound that will be heard by those who have an ear to hear what the Spirit is saying. The church will begin to hear that sound, and God's people will go up together to take the land.

> Then Judah went up, and the LORD delivered the Canaanites and the Perizzites into their hand. (Judges 1:4)

There is a breakthrough anointing that is released into the lives of people who praise God prophetically. But in order to really govern over the heavenlies, you've got to go up! You've got to rise up in the Spirit and take your rightful place in the kingdom. You can't praise from down in the earthly realm, in the middle of your problems and your circumstances. You've got to praise from on high—from the realm of the Spirit, where the blessings and the anointing of God are released. That's the true place where you will be able to govern in the spirit realm. We are seated with Christ in heavenly places.

Have you ever noticed that when you go into a courtroom, the judge is almost always seated higher than the rest of the people? When the judge enters the room and moves to his seat, everyone rises in honor of his office. After the judge sits, everyone else can sit. Our judge, our advocate with the Father, is Christ Jesus. Jesus is at the right hand of the Father, ever

---

6. *Strong's Concordance* #H8085.

interceding for you and me, and He takes his seat there in the heavenly realm. Now, not until Christ's work on the cross, when the veil in the temple was torn in two, had there ever been a priest who was able to take his seat. But because the work is finished—because, on the cross, Jesus said, "It is finished" (John 19:30)—He is now seated at the right hand of the Father. (See, for example, Hebrews 10:12; 12:2.) And because He's seated in heavenly places, we, too, can take our seat in the heavenly places with Him.

The purpose of our being seated in heavenly places is so that we can proceed. We are there to proceed over matters, like a judge.

One definition of proceed is "to move along a course." Do you want to move along a course in your life? Are you tired of spinning your tires? It is important to realize that motion does not necessarily imply progress! You can be in motion and just be going around in circles or just spinning your tires. But God wants you to have forward momentum in your life!

The dictionary provides another definition for proceed: "to continue after a pause or interruption." Do you feel like you've been interrupted lately? Be honest! Sometimes, it feels like you are interrupted just when you seem to be getting somewhere. But God is about to give you momentum to make up for the time that's been lost. You're about to proceed forward! You may not have been getting to where God wants you to go. It may seem like you've lost sight of your purpose in life. But God's about to give you traction. Where it seems you've been stuck and your tires have been spinning, you're about to move forward!

Other definitions for proceed include "to begin and carry on an action, process, or movement," "to go on in an orderly regulated way," and "to come forth from a source." Now, what does it mean in the context of Matthew 4:4, which says, "Man shall not live by bread alone, but by every word that proceeds [begins, comes forth] from the mouth of God"? We can begin to recognize that the word that originated with God is what we must live by! That word comes to us from the throne, and we live by that word. It is our sustenance. That word is how we live.

Another use of the word proceed is especially important; it refers to initiating a legal proceeding against another party. Are you ready to rise up and take legal action against your adversary? This does not mean just praying, "Oh God, please let this happen, if it be Your will." You're not *petitioning*; you are *decreeing*. You are *declaring*. You're passing judgment on your enemy.

Let's take a look at what this means in a verse that's familiar to many Christians today:

> *"No weapon formed against you shall prosper, and every tongue which rises against you in judgment You shall condemn. This is the heritage of the servants of the Lord, and their righteousness is from Me," says the* Lord. (Isaiah 54:17)

This verse literally means that you will pass sentence on—make a declaration or a decree against—your enemies, thereby silencing them! Even if your enemy's weapon is fully formed—even if the enemy gets it all the way built—it will not prosper against you. And every tongue that rises against you in judgment, you will condemn.

> *For though we walk in the flesh, we do not war according to the flesh. For the weapons of our warfare are not carnal but mighty in God for pulling down strongholds, casting down arguments and every high thing that exalts itself against the knowledge of God, bringing every thought into captivity to the obedience of Christ.* (2 Corinthians 10:3–5)

This is the Word of the Lord! God has given you a seat in the heavenlies, and it's your job to pass sentence over the words that the enemy has released concerning your life. The enemy has said to you, "You'll never be anything. You'll never amount to anything. You'll never own anything. You'll never go to any nations. You're never going to fulfill your destiny!" But because these are the words of the enemy, you can know that the exact opposite of what he's said is the truth!

If he told you that you *weren't* going to go to the nations, it should let you know to get your passport ready! If he told you that you would never own a house, you should begin to rejoice, because now you know that you're going to own many houses. He told you that you wouldn't have a car, but get ready—you're about to have three or four cars, because the exact opposite of what he said is true!

But you can't just let those words against your destiny stay up there in the air. When you begin to see those thoughts and imaginations rise up, you have the authority, as a governor of praise, to stand up and silence the enemy. We learned from Psalm 8 that praise releases strength. Out of the mouth of babes He's ordained strength, or praise, so you can silence the mouth of the avenger—so that you might shut the devil up!

The call of the prophet in Jeremiah 1 gives us even further insight:

Then the LORD *put forth His hand and touched my mouth, and the* LORD *said to me: "Behold, I have put My words in your mouth. See, I have this day set you over the nations and over the kingdoms, to root out and to pull down, to destroy and to throw down, to build and to plant."* (Jeremiah 1:9–10)

The word translated as *"set"* in verse 10 comes from a word that means "to be set over." It also means "to be made and overseer," or "to be appointed." The Hebrew word for *set* is *paqad*, which is also translated as "governor." God has appointed you. He's ordained you. He has set you over the nations and kingdoms. Now, this does not just refer the political kingdoms of this world; it also refers to the kingdoms of darkness. It can also mean the kingdoms of the marketplace, or other "kingdoms" in our society today: sports, entertainment, the media, and so forth. God is giving you the authority to reside and to proceed over matters concerning kingdoms—to root out and to pull down, to destroy and to throw down, and to build and to plant. And the good news is that He tells you *how!*

As we have seen, to "proceed" means to institute and conduct legal action. Proceedings include a course of action or a procedure; a sequence of events occurring at a particular place or occasion. It can include legal action or litigation and the instituting or conducting of legal action. God releases His legal action—His authority—to people who rise up in praise.

Governmental anointing is given to those who praise the Lord. Governors of praise are able to rise up and proceed over legal matters. Are you ready to silence the forces of darkness in your region and your life? You can do so when you are a governor of praise. Governors of praise rise up in the ranks. Governors of praise have favor with God and man. Governors of praise don't just sit around waiting for things to happen—they *make* things happen! Governors of praise are leaders. If you want to be a leader, become a governor of praise. If you can't praise God, you don't have any business leading in the church. If you can't praise God, it doesn't matter how talented you are—you don't have anything to say.

On the other hand, when you rise up in praise, you are lining up with the Lion of Judah. You receive the law-giving anointing—the scepter of authority—and you move into heavenly places where you can proceed over legal affairs.

Empowered by the Proceeding Word

According to John 15, there is a proceeding Word that comes from the Father—and that is the Holy Spirit, whom Jesus refers to as "the Helper" in the following passage:

> *Jesus said, "But when the Helper ["Comforter" KJV] comes, whom I shall send to you from the Father, the Spirit of truth who **proceeds** from the Father, He will testify of Me. And you will also bear witness, because you have been with Me from the beginning.*
> (John 15:26–27)

The Spirit of truth proceeds from the Father; the Holy Spirit is a *proceeding Spirit*. He *proceeds* from the Father. He testifies of Jesus—and we do, as well, because we have been with Jesus Himself! Although Jesus was speaking here to the disciples who were with Him in His years on the earth, in the spiritual realm, He was also referring to us, His future disciples.

Jesus said He would send the Comforter Himself. Did you ever stop to realize that the Holy Spirit is a "sent Spirit"? And when you receive this "proceeding Spirit," you receive the proceeding Word. You receive the right to proceed forward and advance, taking authority over the proceedings in your life.

Jesus also said that the Holy Spirit would testify of Him and that we also would bear witness, because we have been with Him from the beginning. How long have you *"been with"* Jesus? You've been with Him from the beginning. You didn't just arrive. You were sent here. You were breathed from the Father into the earth. Before you came to the earth, you were "with Him" in that He was thinking of you, getting ready to create you when and where He wanted to. That's why, every day, you're growing closer to God and moving back into the idea of how things were before you came here. Some people call it déjà vu, but it's not. It's actually something I call a "sonship moment."

Before we were born, God knew we would become His sons. When He created us on earth, forming us in our mother's womb, He created us for such a time as this. There's a legacy that He's been building. Before you were ever born, the Father was breathing things into you. When you were in the lap of the Father, with your head on His chest in the Spirit, He began to release His heartbeat into your life. Then, when you came forth from the birth canal of your mother's womb, when you gave your first cry, He knew what you would become. (See Jeremiah 1.) The Father was intimately involved with you, sowing things into your life. Seeds and spiritual DNA were planted inside of you, and, like a time capsule, they are waiting to open at a certain time. And now, God is beginning to allow those things to erupt in your spirit, and you are beginning to have an understanding of them—even though they were already there before you came into the earth.

God created you for this very time to *proceed* over matters. You didn't just show up. You have legal access. You have legal rights. You were commissioned by the Father. There's never been a greater time in history. As they look down from heaven, the apostles Paul and Peter and John probably wish they could trade places with us!

We are the generation that has the Internet, Facebook, and Twitter, and we can touch the world with the push of a button. We can talk to the world with one camera that operates via satellites. We have smartphones, and we can talk to virtually anyone in the world at any time. Generations ago, it took years to get the Word to remote places across the globe. Today, it can happen instantaneously. We're a chosen generation—chosen to proceed over legal matters in the Spirit.

Changing the World with Proceeding Praise

Thank the Lord for His Word, which teaches us about His prophetic praise that can change the circumstances in our lives and in our world! We have talked about the proceeding Word—God's Holy Spirit—but did you know that there are also proceeding words? Again, Jesus said in Matthew 4:4, *"Man shall not live by bread alone, but by every word that proceeds from the mouth of God."* You and I, and every other person in the world, are each a proceeding word from the Father. You're here because you were spoken into existence. The Bible says that when God spoke, the things He created were *"good"* (see Genesis 1:4, 10, 12, 18, 21, 25), but when He created man, it was *"very good"* (Genesis 1:31). When you were spoken into existence, that same creative power was placed inside of you so that you could tap into heaven's frequency and receive the proceeding Word of the Father. You have the ability to receive the proceeding Word of heaven! And then, as a proceeding word of the Father, you return proceeding praise to Him.

You were not just born; you have a purpose! God spoke you into being. You proceeded out of the very mouth of God and have been sent into the earth for such a time as this. But God has also placed a demand on you—a divine assignment that only *you* can fulfill. He draws you to Himself. The Bible says that no man can come unless he is "drawn" by the Spirit: *"No one can come to Me unless the Father who sent Me draws him"* (John 6:44).

God draws you, and then you follow after Him—His plans and purposes for your life. The Holy Spirit begins to woo you, and as you draw near to Him, He will draw near to you. (See James 4:8.)

God places the proceeding praise in our mouths, and it will cause a release—not of His *rain* but of His *reign* in the earth.

> *And you shall remember that the LORD your God led you all the way these forty years in the wilderness, to humble you and test you, to know what was in your heart, whether you would keep His commandments or not. So He humbled you, allowed you to hunger, and fed you with manna which you did not know nor did your fathers know, that He might make you know that man shall not live by bread alone; but man lives by every word that proceeds from the mouth of the LORD.*
>
> (Deuteronomy 8:2–3)

This is the passage of Scripture Jesus quoted when He was being tempted by satan in the wilderness. (See Matthew 4:1–11; Luke 4:1–12.) Man does not live by bread (earthly food) alone; we need the proceeding Word from God. We need to take that proceeding Word from the heavenlies, transform it into praise, and watch change take place in our lives. The currency of heaven is praise. When you praise God, it causes the kingdom "reign" to fall upon the earth. As soon as God's Word proceeds to earth, it is transformed into praise through God's living vessels— His proceeding words—and then it has the right to take dominion and to bring about change. Your circumstances must bow when proceeding praise is released through your lips!

The Message bible puts Matthew 4:4 like this: "*It takes more than bread to stay alive. It takes a steady stream of words from God's mouth.*" We all need a "*steady stream of words from God's mouth*"! We need more than just a little dab here and there—we need a steady, ongoing, daily stream of words from God, which we then transform into proceeding praise and change our world for His glory!

Proceeding praise is based on the overflow. Revelation 22:1 states, "*And he showed me a pure river of water of life, clear as crystal, proceeding from the throne of God and of the Lamb.*" God's proceeding Word is like a river. The Bible says many times that when God spoke, His voice was like the sound of many waters. (See, for example, Ezekiel 43:2.) When

God speaks, His glory sounds like thunder crashing through the spiritual realm. It changes things! It shakes things up! It is like a thunderstorm from heaven about to release the rains of overflow into your life. When you begin to experience the sound of His voice, the overflow will come. Not only will your bills be paid, but there will also be money left over to sow into the work of the kingdom. Not only will your children be saved, but their children and their children will come to salvation, as well. You will see mountains move and strongholds pulled down, so that God may be fully glorified in your life.

5

GOING TO WAR!

But thou, O Daniel, shut up the words, and seal the book, even to the time of the end: many shall run to and fro, and knowledge shall be increased. (Daniel 12:4 KJV)

The Bible says that in the last days, people are going to be running around the globe like crazy and that knowledge is going to increase. As you follow the Lord in these last days, is there any doubt that life seems to be going faster and faster? There's no way to keep up with all the new discoveries in every area of life.

Technology has connected the world so that what happens in China is known in America within seconds. You can travel anywhere in the world within hours. You can fill your days with endless activities, or connect to the world through Facebook and the Internet on your laptop, iPad, or smartphone.

Believers are seeing the fulfillment of prophecy at an accelerated rate, as well.

Then said the Lord unto me, Thou hast well seen: for I will hasten my
word to perform it. (Jeremiah 1:12 KJV)

God is saying, in effect, "I will speed up, or accelerate, the perfor-
mance of My Word." Let's look at the definitions of *accelerate*:

1. To bring about at an earlier time.

2. To cause to move faster.

3. To hasten the progress or development of.

God can shorten the interval between the present time and future
events, so as to accelerate the ruin of a government, for example. In the
last days, God is going to move faster and faster in fulfilling His promises.
He's going to continually increase the speed at which He acts. He's going
to do this supernaturally and miraculously. He is going to shorten the
length of time that it would ordinarily take to do something.

Six Steps of Acceleration

We must go back to Jeremiah 1 to discover *how* things are accelerated.

See, I have this day set you over the nations and over the kingdoms, to
root out and to pull down, to destroy and to throw down, to build and
to plant. (Jeremiah 1:10)

This verse of Scripture spells out the function and mandate of the
apostle and prophet today:

1. to root out,

2. to pull down,

3. to destroy,

4. to throw down,

5. to build, and

6. to plant.

What happens when I'm not seeing my promise fulfilled? It's time to throw Jezebel off the train! It's time to jump on the enemy and root out some things.

If you're in a situation that's messed up, you've got to pull down the strongholds, destroy the work of the enemy, and begin building that which God desires in its place. When we fulfill these six steps, we usher in heaven on earth, resulting in the acceleration of the fulfillment of God's promises. The six keys found in Jeremiah 1:10 unlock lasting breakthrough in cities, regions, and nations.

Destroying the Work of the Enemy

The first four keys deal with spiritual warfare. We know from Ephesians 6:10–18 that you cannot even put on the armor of God without purifying yourself first. The first piece of armor is the belt of truth. Not only does this refer to believing God's Word, but it also speaks of honesty. If you are going to go to war in the spirit realm, you had better come clean and be brutally honest with God about your life.

Why is this so important? Because satan knows your weaknesses, your past sins, and everything you struggle with. He also knows everything you sweep under the rug and refuse to deal with. And when you are in the heat of battle, he will pull these things out and shoot you down with them. He will render you powerless and hopeless because of your own faults, sins, and disobedience. Can you see why the first key on the list of steps for acceleration is to root out? Apostles and prophets put a demand on the body of Christ to root out, pull down, destroy, and throw down carnality, worldliness, and demonic influence. I believe this is why there is a great wave of repentance moving through churches today. As the apostles and prophets are set in place, the Holy Spirit flows through them to purify the church and prepare her for war—a war that causes heaven to come to earth and accelerates the fulfillment of God's promises.

Root Out

The Hebrew word for this key is *nathash*, which means "to pull up, expel, pluck up."[7] Before we can root out the works of darkness in cities, regions, and nations, we have to root out the works of darkness in our own lives and churches.

> *Leave no [such] room or foothold for the devil [give no opportunity to him].*   (Ephesians 4:27 AMP)

Satan cannot and will not cast out himself. If you are "sleeping with the enemy," he doesn't have to submit to your authority. In fact, when it comes down to it, you really don't have authority until he has no room in your inn!

In dealing with spiritual root systems, we must remember to dig deep. Like cutting down trees or removing weeds and other unwanted plants, if the whole root system is not removed, it will grow back. Too many times, believers deal only with the fruit of the problem. They stay on the surface and wonder why they are seeing no lasting victory over areas of sin and weakness.

It is often painful to dig deep and face our greatest doubts, fears, sins, and past trauma, but it must be done if we are to be free of the enemy's hold. We must get to the root of the problem. Then, through repentance and spiritual warfare, we can rid ourselves of satan's bitter fruit forever.

Pull Down

The Hebrew word for "pull down," *nathats*, means "to...break down, cast down, throw down, beat down, destroy, overthrow, break out."[8]

When we are brutally honest about ourselves with God and get to the root of the problem, it is time to employ the weapons of our warfare to defeat the enemy. Once satan is defeated in our personal lives and in our local church, then we can defeat him for good in the territories and nations of the earth.

---

7. *Strong's Concordance* #H5428.
8. *Strong's Concordance* #H5422.

We use God's mighty weapons, not [mere] worldly weapons, to knock down the [devil's] strongholds.... (2 Corinthians 10:4 NLT)

One of the first times my eyes were opened to the warfare that takes place over people's lives occurred when I received a vision in the fall of 1988. I was playing drums in a praise band, and when I clanged the cymbals together, one of my drumsticks became a huge sword in the Spirit. There were cords streaming down from the heavens and passing through the ceiling of the auditorium, attaching themselves to some of the people in the service. As I continued to play the drums, the sword cut through those cords of darkness and pulled them down.

Then I had a vision of a young couple I had never seen before. The Lord revealed what they were going through and how they were bound by the enemy. I continued to play, but I also began interceding for this couple. Within minutes, they walked in through the back door! I had to rub my eyes a couple of times to make sure I wasn't seeing things. I put down my drumsticks and gave an altar call, and this young couple came forward. When I ministered to them according to the vision I'd had, they were set free and saved! Glory to God!

Every time we engage in spiritual warfare and use this key of pulling down strongholds, we will experience new dimensions of liberty and clarity.

For though we walk in the flesh, we do not war after the flesh: (For the weapons of our warfare are not carnal, but mighty through God to the pulling down of strong holds;) casting down imaginations, and every high thing that exalteth itself against the knowledge of God, and bringing into captivity every thought to the obedience of Christ; and having in a readiness to revenge all disobedience, when your obedience is fulfilled. (2 Corinthians 10:3–6 KJV)

Apostles and prophets are people of war. Battling for souls in the spirit realm is normal, everyday life to them. The Greek word for *"warfare"* in 2 Corinthians 10:4 is *strateia*, from which we get the English word *strategy*.

It means "an expedition, campaign, military service, i.e. (figuratively) the apostolic career (as one of hardship and danger)—warfare." God has given apostles the job of raising up people through strategic prayer so that they can possess the land and bring people to Jesus Christ.

The apostle Paul is telling us that part of his apostolic career and duty is to engage in strategic spiritual warfare and to train others to do the same. Strategic warfare is part of our apostolic career. It's time for the church to enter into battle against the forces of darkness with the host of heaven. Every believer has a battle station to occupy.

> *This charge I commit to you, son Timothy, according to the prophecies previously made concerning you, that by them you may wage the good warfare.* (1 Timothy 1:18)

According to Ephesians 6:17, your sword is the Word of God; but, according to 1 Timothy 1:18, it is also the prophetic word of the Lord you receive to fight the good fight of faith. Remember, the Bible says that the Word of God is sharper than a two-edged sword. (See Hebrews 4:12.) Take up the prophecies and God's Word and wield them as a sword. Declare and decree what the Lord has said in order to wage effective warfare.

The two-edged sword also makes a double impact in war. While God's Word and His prophecies to you serve as a ramrod to break through into the manifestation and demonstration of what God has promised you, they are also working to pull down the enemy's strongholds.

Destroy

The Hebrew word for *"destroy"* even sounds bad! It is *abad*, which means "perish, vanish, go, astray, be destroyed."[9]

This is the most picturesque definition of this word I have found. *Abad* is used to describe the downfall of nations, the withering away of crops, and the fading away of strength, hope, wisdom, knowledge, and wealth. It is applied to the destruction of temples, images, and pictures. It suggests utter defeat (see Joshua 7:7), the overthrow of a nation (see Deuteronomy 28:51),

---

9. *Strong's Concordance* #H6.

and the taking of a life. *Abad* can also mean "to be lost, to lose oneself, to wander, especially used as a lost and wandering sheep."

This is a violent word! God is raising up holy destroyers to leave the enemy's works desolate. It will take nothing less than an all-out righteous assault on satan and his hordes to see lasting breakthrough in the earth. When we are finished with them, *they* should be wandering around aimlessly without orientation, powerless to do anything on the earth.

The church will either destroy or be destroyed, because the enemy will not stop unless we stop him.

> *The thief cometh not, but for to steal, and to kill, and to destroy.*
> (John 10:10 KJV)

I have come across many believers who prefer to live in ignorance of spiritual warfare. For them, everything is all right as long as everything is all right! It has hurt my heart to see some of these people go through devastation and loss because they refused to engage in strategic spiritual warfare.

I made up my mind a long time ago that I was not going to be a punching bag or a doormat for the enemy. If he ever comes to my door, I'm ready! The Lion of the Tribe of Judah will roar through me, "You rang?" These days, I wake up in the morning looking to destroy the works of darkness. I ask the Holy Spirit to show me someone to snatch from the fire or someone to whom I can minister healing or deliverance.

There is a movie that epitomizes the attitude of aggression we in the church must have to defeat the enemy. *Enough* is the story about a battered wife who takes her child and leaves her abusive husband to run for her life. Throughout the movie, her husband tries to find her and kill her. Going through one close call after another, the wife finally decides to stop being the victim—the one who's being chased down—and chooses to go on the offensive. She discovers that her husband is planning to kill her while she is in town for a custody hearing. If she doesn't attend the hearing, the judge will rule that her daughter will have to live with the abusive father.

So, she wises up, enrolls in martial arts classes, and begins to strategize on how to take her enemy out on his own turf.

She manages to escape the creeps her husband hired to follow her, and flies to the city where he lives. She breaks into his house while he's out and prepares to ambush him. This lady is bad to the bone! She cuts the phone lines, installs a system that blocks cell phone signals, rearranges the furniture, and rigs the lights to come on and go right back off. Then she oils herself down so that if he strikes her, the blows will slide off of her. She laces up her steel-toed boots, puts on some brass knuckles, and waits for her enemy.

When he comes home, he doesn't know what hit him! It's just like those old Batman shows. *Pow! Bam!* Not to endorse violence between people, but, for me, this is a picture of the bride of Christ doing warfare against the enemy, being so strong that the devil doesn't know what hit him. He's left to wander around the earth, totally disoriented, lost, and desolate.

It's time for God's children to declare, "Enough!" It's time to fulfill the mission of Jesus Christ, meet the enemy on his own turf, and take him out! It's time to get oiled down with the anointing of the Holy Spirit, so that nothing the enemy tries to pull on us will work!

> *The yoke will be destroyed because of the anointing oil.*
> (Isaiah 10:27)

It's time for us to put on the whole armor of God and knock the enemy down, in Jesus' name!

Throw Down

The Hebrew word in Jeremiah 1:10 for *"throw down"* is *harac*, meaning "to tear down, break down, overthrow, beat down, break, break through, destroy, pluck down, pull down,…ruin, destroy utterly."

> *For the weapons of our warfare are not carnal but mighty in God for pulling down strongholds.* (2 Corinthians 10:4)

Once you have rooted out, pulled down, and destroyed the enemy, it's time to throw him down. It's one thing to beat the tar out of the enemy; it's another thing to dethrone the enemy and send him packing! It's one thing to win a few battles; it's another thing to win the war. If you've fought this hard for this long, you might as well go ahead and have some fun with it!

Take your seat in heavenly places with Christ Jesus; gather up all the roots, cords, and strongholds of the enemy; and then throw them down. Enforce the work of Jesus by completely stripping the principalities and powers, rulers of the darkness of this world, and spiritual wickedness in high places of all authority over cities, regions, and nations. Hallelujah!

The work of God's apostles and prophets is only half finished, but even now, you can see how the fulfillment of God's Word is accelerated when the body of Christ declares war on the enemy and fights him strategically. In the next chapter, you will see how heaven is released on earth and how the acceleration increases when God's presence and government are set in place through the final two steps of acceleration: *building* and *planting*.

6

SECURING SPIRITUAL BEACHHEADS

See, I have this day set you over the nations and over the kingdoms, to root out and to pull down, to destroy and to throw down, to build and to plant. (Jeremiah 1:10)

Many historians believe that World War II was won because the Allied troops established a beachhead in Normandy, enabling them to deliver ammunition, food, equipment, and reinforcements to support their invasion further into Europe.

The apostle Paul always established a ministry beachhead. In each town or city, he would develop a core of believers and a strategic place of operation to reach the entire area God had called him to. This was a safe haven where the transference of power from the kingdom of darkness to the kingdom of light could begin as the reign of the Prince of Peace was inaugurated in that region.

In taking territory for God, after the enemy has been rooted out, pulled down, destroyed, and thrown down, the apostles and prophets must establish a beachhead of peace to spread the good news of the Prince of Peace and to continue to wage war for souls. Unfortunately, because there have been few apostles and prophets, the church has established few beachheads. As a result, the kingdom of God has suffered loss. Tragically, we have lost believers—casualties of war who are often young in the Lord. Many such losses could be avoided if prophetic strategies would be initiated by the apostolic authorities in place.

Have you ever wondered why so many believers seem to take two steps forward and three steps backward? Perhaps you have even felt this way yourself. Have you found yourself asking, *Why am I going through this same battle, over and over again?*

In the 1980s, during a resurgence of the truths of spiritual warfare, we pulled down a lot of strongholds, but we didn't build and plant in the places where those strongholds had been uprooted. Therefore, the enemy came right back after we'd left our prophetic prayer meetings and praise rallies and found the house empty. As a result, things often got worse than before we had prayed!

As usual, God's Word has the answer for us.

> *When an unclean spirit goes out of a man, he goes through dry places, seeking rest, and finds none. Then he says, "I will return to my house from which I came." And when he comes, he finds it empty, swept, and put in order. Then he goes and takes with him seven other spirits more wicked than himself, and they enter and dwell there; and the last state of that man is worse than the first. So shall it also be with this wicked generation.* (Matthew 12:43–45)

Jesus was speaking of an individual who is delivered and then filled with God's Word, only to backslide and be filled with even more demonic spirits than before. His words are for our generation, as well. There is generational repentance and deliverance; there is corporate repentance and deliverance. The liberation of Europe by the Allied troops to end

World War II is a great example of corporate deliverance in the natural realm.

Doing the Work of God

The presence of God—and His order and government—must *replace* the principalities and powers, the rulers of the darkness of this world, and the spiritual wickedness in high places over cities, regions, and nations that have been dethroned and defeated. Otherwise, the ground that was taken in war cannot be maintained in peace. To achieve this, God uses apostles and prophets of praise to build and to plant where the enemy once reigned.

Build

In the Hebrew, the word translated as *"build"* in Jeremiah 1:10 is *banah*, meaning "to rebuild, establish, cause to continue."[10] Earlier, we saw how apostles are to be fathers in the faith, called to raise up sons who will be faithful to war, worship, and work for the Lord. This is part of the building that the apostles undertake. The following verses refer to both natural and spiritual sons and daughters:

> *Behold, children are a heritage from the Lord, the fruit of the womb is a reward. Like arrows in the hand of a warrior, so are the children of one's youth. Happy is the man who has his quiver full of them; they shall not be ashamed, but shall speak with their enemies in the gate.*
> (Psalm 127:3–5)

These sons and daughters *"speak with their enemies in the gate."* The gate is the seat of government in a city or territory. And the Hebrew word for *"speak"* is *dabar*, meaning "to declare, converse, command, promise, warn."[11] These definitions speak of governmental authority.

> *In blessing I will bless thee, and in multiplying I will multiply thy seed as the stars of the heaven, and as the sand which is upon the sea shore;*

---

10. *Strong's Concordance* #H1129.
11. *Strong's Concordance* #H1696.

and thy seed shall possess the gate of his enemies; and in thy seed shall all the nations of the earth be blessed; because thou hast obeyed my voice. (Genesis 22:17–18 KJV)

In this passage of Scripture, God is telling Abraham that he will have spiritual seed (the church) and natural seed (the nation of Israel). Believers produce natural seed and spiritual seed—natural sons and daughters and spiritual sons and daughters. God willing, our natural seed will serve God and thereby be the same as our spiritual seed. They will literally *"possess the gate of* [our] *enemies."*

Listen, O coastlands, to Me, and take heed, you peoples from afar! The LORD has called Me from the womb; from the matrix of My mother He has made mention of My name. And He has made My mouth like a sharp sword; in the shadow of His hand He has hidden Me, and made Me a polished shaft; in His quiver He has hidden Me. And He said to Me, "You are My servant, O Israel, in whom I will be glorified." (Isaiah 49:1–3)

Like Jesus, the apostles' sons and daughters do spiritual warfare to affect nations so that the harvest of souls can be reaped. The governmental authority of the apostles releases these gifts like arrows.

In Judges 6, Gideon tore down the altars of Baal and built an altar to the Lord. In spiritual warfare, we tear down the strongholds of the enemy and build altars to the Lord in their place.

For he took away the altars of the strange gods, and the high places, and brake down the images, and cut down the groves: and commanded Judah to seek the LORD God of their fathers, and to do the law and the commandment. Also he took away out of all the cities of Judah the high places and the images: and the kingdom was quiet before him. And he built fenced cities in Judah: for the land had rest, and he had no war in those years; because the LORD had given him rest. Therefore he said unto Judah, Let us build these cities, and make about them walls, and towers, gates, and bars, while the land is yet before us;

because we have sought the Lord our God, we have sought him, and
he hath given us rest on every side. So they built and prospered.

(2 Chronicles 14:3–7 KJV)

The essence of apostolic building is found in prayer and worship, which we will cover in later chapters. But you can see from this passage in 2 Chronicles that building altars to the Lord establishes peace and brings prosperity. The apostles and prophets are the governmental foundation that bring God's presence and order into the land through prayer and worship. Their praise releases heaven on earth, giving supernatural acceleration for the fulfillment of the Word of the Lord.

Why? Because the land is now inhabited by God rather than by the forces of darkness.

But thou art holy, O thou that inhabitest the praises of Israel.

(Psalm 22:3 KJV)

Plant

The Hebrew word for *"plant"* in Jeremiah 1:10 is *nata*, meaning "to fashion, fix, establish." It is to strike something into the ground so deeply that it is fastened there forever. There is one weapon of our warfare that is especially effective: the sword of the Spirit, which pulls out the enemy's strongholds by the roots, making room for God's truth to be planted deeply in the land.

And I have put My words in your mouth; I have covered you with the
shadow of My hand, that I may plant the heavens, lay the foundations
of the earth, and say to Zion, "You are My people."   (Isaiah 51:16)

When we proclaim God's Word, we are planting heaven on earth! Angels are waiting for us to speak His Word so they can assist us. And notice that God puts His words in our mouths. This is referring to *prophetic proclamation*. We are to *proclaim* and declare the prophetic words of the Lord. We are to *prophesy* His will and wisdom into the earth.

Proactive Faith Brings Heaven to Earth

Apostolic believers continually "get in the face" of the enemy and declare, "You're not going to have my stuff. You're not going to have my blessings. You're not robbing my family members, my neighbors, or my coworkers of their salvation. Get off my land. Get out of my territory. I'm a child of the King, and this is the King's domain!"

When we get "fed up with the setup" and begin to deal with the enemy, heaven comes to earth, and acceleration occurs. Pacifists who wait for a blessing will never see it. If you want to accelerate the arrival of your promises, you have to accelerate yourself in faith. You have to put your foot on the Word and move in the Spirit. Pick up the pace of the race. Prophesy. Pray in the Spirit.

Acceleration comes when we stand in faith and release what God is saying in this hour. He sees our faith, and His heart leaps! He doesn't see our need—He sees our faith.

Faith Brings Acceleration

God is not moved by our needs but by our faith. I could take you all over the world to places where people are in need, and you would clearly see that God does not seem to be moved by their needs, because nothing is happening. But when somebody arises in the midst of those people, with faith in the midst of the need, God responds to that faith. And so it is with you and me.

Are you getting stressed about your situation? Maybe it's your finances, your health, or your job. Imagine you're in the ocean, swimming toward your destination. Your stress is sending blood into the water, and sharks (satan's demons) are circling you. When demons see fear, doubt, unbelief, and stress, they attack.

You have to go to war and release that stress to God—root it out, pull it down, destroy it, and throw it down—and then build an altar of worship and plant the Word of God by declaring that you're too blessed to be stressed!

The Bible declares in Romans 10:17 that faith comes by hearing God's Word. It also tells you in Jude 20 that praying in the Spirit causes faith to rise up in your spirit. So, fill yourself with the Word of God and pray in tongues to defeat stress and worry. You're filled with the Holy Spirit. You have God's Word. And if God is for you, who can be against you? (See Romans 8:31.)

If God is in you, you can be confident, because He is greater than the devil and all his demons. There has to be a stirring inside of you. Your spirit-man may be crying out, "I know this looks bad right now, but, just like Paul and Silas, I'm going to have faith. I'm going to sing and praise God in the midst of this situation, and He will turn it around."

I know your religious mind is arguing with me. You're looking at your situation and thinking, *Well, I haven't come into anything but a bunch of pain and debt and trouble. I don't know what's going on.*

I'm going to tell you the truth: If you continue to keep that mind-set, you will wander in the desert like the children of Israel. If all this preaching and teaching only incites you to argue with the Word of God, you'll be prone to wander, and God will have to raise up another one like you to grab ahold of His Word, believe His promises, and go forward.

None of us is the "only one." God will say, "Saul, move out of the way; it's time for a David to arise. Eli, go; it's time for a Samuel to arise!" He will choose another person. God's kingdom is not hinging on you fulfilling your divine destiny. God's kingdom is sure. If you don't fulfill your destiny, there will be lives that will not be touched, and there will be things that you should have done that could not have been done without you, but God's kingdom will still stand strong.

The children of Israel did not believe. Instead, they complained and wandered, but that didn't negate the promise of God that Israel would possess the Promised Land. There was a generation that had to pass away. And I'm concerned in my spirit when I see the word of the Lord comes to someone who agrees with it but then grows frustrated when he does not see immediate results. Eventually, he succumbs to unbelief. He is just like the children of Israel who weren't allowed to go into the Promised Land.

"Today, if you will hear His voice, do not harden your hearts as in the rebellion." For who, having heard, rebelled? Indeed, was it not all who came out of Egypt, led by Moses? Now with whom was He angry forty years? Was it not with those who sinned, whose corpses fell in the wilderness? And to whom did He swear that they would not enter His rest, but to those who did not obey? So we see that they could not enter in because of unbelief. (Hebrews 3:15–19)

Engaging in spiritual warfare and building and planting to maintain peace all take patience and faith. There's a process to obtain the promise. Sometimes, you have to go through difficult times to get something and to go someplace. If there's no test, there will be no testimony. If there's no trial, there's no reason to use your faith. Don't run from place to place, ignoring the instruction and correction of the Lord.

The Bible says that in the last days, there will be a famine of the hearing of the Word of the Lord. (See Amos 8:11.) It doesn't say there will be a famine of the Word of the Lord. It says there will be a famine of the *hearing* of the Word of the Lord. That means people who don't want to hear the Word of God, or the prophetic words He wants to give them, will run and find somebody else who will tell them what they want to hear. This is the opposite of apostolic order! (See 2 Timothy 4:3–4.)

The Bible says that God hastens—or accelerates—to *perform* His Word.

God doesn't hasten to perform His Word for those who refuse to war.

God doesn't hasten to perform His Word for those who will not build or plant.

God doesn't hasten to perform His Word for those who sit and wait for things to happen.

God doesn't hasten to perform His Word for those who complain.

God doesn't hasten to perform His Word for those who doubt and fall into unbelief.

God doesn't hasten to perform His Word for those who are moved by what they see.

God hastens to perform His Word—there is acceleration to the fulfillment of His promises—for those who walk in proactive faith. Through all the rooting out, pulling down, destroying, throwing down, building, and planting, they move forward, believing that God watches over His Word to perform it.

Your Daily Role in Acceleration

If you want to see God hasten His Word to perform it in your life, there are some things you need to do. We've talked about apostolic access and the importance of coming into order and unity in the body of Christ. We've seen the apostolic function of defeating the enemy and building the kingdom of God. When that happens, God hastens His Word to perform it. But each believer has a vital role to perform.

How much time are you spending in prayer?

How much time are you spending in praise and worship?

How much time are you fasting?

How much time are you standing before God, saying, "Lord, I want to see this Word come to pass"?

Do you believe the prophetic utterances that have been spoken over your life, and are you bombarding the heavens with them?

Are you dispatching angels, or are your angels just sitting in a corner, twiddling their thumbs?

What are you doing with the things God has given you—gifts, talents, and resources?

If you'll agree with God's Word and the prophetic words about your life, you're going to see momentum in His promises being fulfilled.

You venture higher through prayer, praise, and meditation on God's Word. You penetrate the heavens and execute change in the spirit realm by prayer, praise, and prophecy in the presence of God. And when you do this, you step into another dimension of God's power and glory, and things begin to speed up in the natural realm.

The Word of God tells us, "*These signs will follow those who believe*" (Mark 16:17). It doesn't say these signs will follow Kathryn Kuhlman, Benny Hinn, or Smith Wigglesworth exclusively. If you'll get passionate and aggressive in prayer, praise, and the study of God's Word, you'll see acceleration come to your calling and destiny. Next year, when you look back, you're going to see how those things that eluded you in the past have come into your hands.

There are believers who are about to go into warp speed. I feel it! Some are about to take quantum leaps in God. As you spend time in His presence and agree with His Word, you're going to break through the walls that have been holding you back. Then, nothing will be able to resist you, because you will have apostolic access *and* acceleration.

7

POISED FOR POSSESSION

.

At midnight Paul and Silas prayed, and sang praises unto God: and the prisoners heard them. And suddenly there was a great earthquake, so that the foundations of the prison were shaken: and immediately all the doors were opened, and every one's bands were loosed.

(Acts 16:25–26 KJV)

God's Time Twins: *Suddenly* and *Immediately*

As you arise like Paul and Silas, God will release His "time twins": *Suddenly* and *Immediately*, which open doors to opportunity and breakthrough. *Suddenly* is going to shift things, and *Immediately* is going to open doors! You're going to walk through doors that have been shut and experience favor like never before.

Suddenly and *Immediately* are about to rain on the devil's parade. He thought he had you up against the wall, but *Immediately* is coming to open the door and loose you from whatever binds you.

Are you tired of being bound? Are you tired of seeing your family, friends, and nation bound?

> *And the keeper of the prison awaking from sleep, and seeing the prison doors open, he drew out his sword, and would have killed himself, supposing that the prisoners had been fled. But Paul called with a loud voice, saying, Do thyself no harm: for we are all here. Then he called for a light, and sprang in, and came trembling, and fell down before Paul and Silas, and brought them out, and said, Sirs, what must I do to be saved? And they said, Believe on the Lord Jesus Christ, and thou shalt be saved, and thy house. And they spake unto him the word of the Lord, and to all that were in his house. And he took them the same hour of the night, and washed their stripes; and was baptized, he and all his, straightway.* (Acts 16:27–33 KJV)

Again, when *Suddenly* and *Immediately* show up, souls are saved and bonds are loosed! I don't know what you're going through, but *Suddenly* and *Immediately* are about to work as a tag team and hop on the devil for you. They're going to take care of that circumstance or situation.

You may be thinking, *Well, Joshua, you haven't been through anything. Everything goes great for you. You don't have any problems. You just write books and preach, and people get all excited and give you lots of money.*

This is what happens when you're a preacher—people don't think you have any problems or needs. They don't believe you've had to live what you preach. Well, I have been through some things, and I can tell you what *not* to do!

Disobedience Causes Delay

Have you ever been restrained? You haven't been restrained until you've been restrained by God. God has taken me through some hard times. We were living in a city where we were preaching on the radio, making dynamic music, winning lots of souls for Jesus, and living in a nice house. Then God moved us to another city, sat me down, and told me not to do anything. "Don't start a church; don't call a meeting; don't go anywhere and preach; don't get a job. I'll provide for you."

At that time, I had two houses in two different cities to pay for, a wife and children to feed and clothe, and no income. You're probably thinking that the ravens fed us, like they fed Elijah beside the brook (see 1 Kings 17:4–6)—that birds just dropped money from the sky to pay my rent. Or maybe that I went out to my money tree every day and picked cash from the branches.

That didn't happen.

You probably are thinking that somebody I prophesied or prayed over, somebody that I blessed during all the years of traveling throughout America and the nations, got a revelation from God and sent me some money.

That didn't happen, either.

Finally, when the bills were past due and I needed God to show up, we received a call to minister, and the Lord provided enough money to cover both house payments and all of our bills! We all rejoiced like crazy, but there was still that frustration: *God, why didn't You do that three days ago?*

Have you ever been there?

That's when the Holy Spirit revealed to me that disobedience causes delays—it holds up your *Suddenly* and *Immediately*. There were things that God had told me to do, but, for whatever reason, I kept putting them off. And my procrastination in obeying was contagious. The Lord showed me that there were several people He had tapped on the shoulder and asked to send me money, but they hadn't done it. It wasn't too hard to see what had happened. Because I didn't do something for somebody else, those who were supposed to do something for me didn't do it. You reap what you sow!

My wife and I decided that from that point on, if God told us to do something, we were going to do it, right then and there. If He awakened us in the middle of the night and told us to give someone a hundred dollars, we'd go to the person's house that night. Why? Because we wanted to move into a season of *Suddenly* and *Immediately*. Since making this commitment, we have experienced tremendous blessing and favor in our lives.

Disbelief Robs Us of Our Blessing

> *Elisha said, "Hear the word of the* LORD*. This is what the* LORD *says: About this time tomorrow, a seah of flour will sell for a shekel and two seahs of barley for a shekel at the gate of Samaria."*
>
> (2 Kings 7:1 NIV)

In 2 Kings 6, we read a most horrifying story. There was such poverty and famine in the land that some people were eating their own children. It's hard to fathom such hopelessness and despair.

In the midst of all this poverty and difficulty, the prophet Elisha prophesied that *"about this time tomorrow,"* things were going to change. He told the people to get ready, because things were about to turn around! They were going to move from poverty to prosperity, from lack to abundance.

Like many religious people of our day, there was an unbeliever in the midst who spoke up and expressed his feelings of doubt and unbelief. The prophet told him, "You will see it, but you won't access it." The word of the Lord, spoken through the prophet, came to pass, and the people experienced a breakthrough the very next day!

What happened to the unbeliever? He saw the fulfillment of the word, but he did not partake of it.

> *Now the king had put the officer on whose arm he leaned in charge of the gate, and the people trampled him in the gateway, and he died, just as the man of God had foretold when the king came down to his house. It happened as the man of God had said to the king: "About this time tomorrow, a seah of flour will sell for a shekel and two seahs of barley for a shekel at the gate of Samaria." The officer had said to the man of God, "Look, even if the* LORD *should open the floodgates of the heavens, could this happen?" The man of God had replied, "You will see it with your own eyes, but you will not eat any of it!" And that is exactly*

what happened to him, for the people trampled him in the gateway, and he died. (2 Kings 7:17–20 NIV)

If you desire to partake of the promises of God, you must believe Him and those He sends to speak into your life.

We see with 20/20 vision God's plan for our lives in 2 Chronicles 20:20. The Word declares, *"Believe in the LORD your God, and you shall be established; believe His prophets, and you shall prosper."*

When we believe God's prophets, we prosper. There are too many "non-prophet" organizations in the church today! Because they are "non-prophet," they also are nonprofit. They profit little for the kingdom of God because they won't receive or listen to God's apostles and prophets. Let's be like those in 2 Kings 7 who believed, and we will enter into the dimension called *"about this time tomorrow"*!

Prepare for Possession

And I will give unto thee the keys of the kingdom of heaven: and whatsoever thou shalt bind on earth shall be bound in heaven: and whatsoever thou shalt loose on earth shall be loosed in heaven.
(Matthew 16:19 KJV)

The key of the house of David I will lay on his shoulder; so he shall open, and no one shall shut; and he shall shut, and no one shall open.
(Isaiah 22:22)

The Master Key: The Tabernacle of David

Have you ever asked yourself why so many people seem unable to possess their God-given promises? Have you grown tired of religious reruns and merry-go-round ministries? Are you asking the same question as the elderly lady in that old Wendy's commercial, "Where's the beef?"

Where's the harvest?

Where are the signs and wonders, miracles, and healings?

Why are there so many empty seats in churches today?

If these are the questions you are asking, you are in the company of those like me, who have experienced a holy dissatisfaction for wasting time wandering aimlessly in the wilderness.

Child of God, you were called to possess! You have not come to the kingdom for such a time as this to be a wilderness-walker. You have been chosen to enter in and possess the land! You are called to be a promise-possessor!

How can we release heaven on earth? How can we arise and possess the land? How will the church enter into the anointing to gather the greatest harvest of all time? According to the Word of God, we open doors with the key of David, and through rebuilding the tabernacle of David, we position ourselves for possession.

> *"On that day I will raise up the tabernacle of David, which has fallen down, and repair its damages; I will raise up its ruins, and rebuild it as in the days of old; that they may possess the remnant of Edom, and all the Gentiles who are called by My name," says the* LORD *who does this thing.* (Amos 9:11–12)

> *After this I will come back, and will rebuild the house of David,…so that the rest of men may seek the Lord.* (Acts 15:16–17 AMP)

These Scriptures vividly reveal that once we set out to co-labor with Jesus in building the tabernacle of David, we will enter into an unprecedented anointing for reaping a harvest of souls. Revelation abounds to me regarding the tabernacle of David, but before I share some of these truths, I need to express the importance of what you are about to read.

8

REBUILDING THE TABERNACLE

In 1998, I began fervently seeking the mind of God for His blueprint for the church. I was pastoring a young church and was desperately longing for His move to come forth. Like many others, I had been hungry to usher in God's design, pattern, and original model for the church. Shortly thereafter, I began teaching a series entitled "Apostolic Blueprints for the 21st Century Church." In this series, I gave an acronym for the word *design* that revealed what I believe to be a major portion of the blueprint for the church.

D.E.S.I.G.N.

D – Davidic Order of Worship and Intercession (rebuilding the tabernacle of David)

E – Elisha's Expression of the Double-Portion Anointing (mentoring, discipleship)

S – Sending Factor

I – International Vision

G – Governments and the Governmental Church

N – Nonconformism (defying the lie of separation of church and state)

What I will share now is a portion of what God revealed to me about the first letter of the acronym: D, or Davidic Order of Worship and Intercession.

In order for us to understand Davidic order, we need to understand what the tabernacle of David is and how it can be rebuilt in our cities and nations. We get a picture of how King David received the pattern for the tabernacle of David in 2 Samuel 6.

> *So they set the ark of God on a new cart, and brought it out of the house of Abinadab, which was on the hill; and Uzzah and Ahio, the sons of Abinadab, drove the new cart....And when they came to Nachon's threshing floor, Uzzah put out his hand to the ark of God and took hold of it, for the oxen stumbled. Then the anger of the LORD was aroused against Uzzah, and God struck him there for his error; and he died there by the ark of God.* (2 Samuel 6:3, 6–7)

Like many "Uzzah-friendly" churches are finding out today, David learned the hard way that you can't bring the presence of God in on a cart!

The "cart" in this story represents mankind's thinking and methods. The cart is found in many churches today in the form of programs, popularity-seeking political agendas, and man's traditions. The death of Uzzah, whose name means "strength," clearly reveals that we cannot harness, dictate, or control the movement of God with our natural strength or abilities.

After Uzzah's death, King David sought the Lord for direction. In 2 Samuel 6:9, David asked, *"How can the ark of the LORD [God's presence] come to me?"* This is a question we should be asking today.

David sent his servants to search the Scriptures for advice on how to move the ark, and we should be doing the same thing today. He discovered that the ark of the Lord—the presence of God—must be carried on the shoulders of the priests. The Word of God declares that once King David set things in order by having the priests carry the ark and make sacrifices to God, he was able to lead all of Israel into the city in a procession of victorious praise. David danced before the Lord with all his might, and the people shouted and played instruments. (See 1 Chronicles 15:26–28; 2 Samuel 6:14.)

Once the ark was safely brought back to Jerusalem, they set it in a tent that David had pitched specifically for this purpose. Then David stationed Levites to minister before the ark of the Lord—the presence of God—to *record, thank,* and *praise* the Lord God of Israel continually—24/7, 365 days a year. (See 1 Chronicles 16:1, 4, 37.)

In these passages of Scripture, we learn that the tabernacle of David was a tent that housed the ark of the Lord. First Chronicles 25:7 says that 288 singers were stationed to minister to the Lord continually in intercession, praise, and worship.

Perhaps you are asking yourself if the tabernacle of David is really for today, and, if so, how can we rebuild it? Yes, it is for today. Starting with King David and his son Solomon, this pattern has been handed down as an eternal, heavenly pattern.

> *Then David gave his son Solomon the plans for the vestibule, its houses, its treasuries, its upper chambers, its inner chambers, and the place of the mercy seat; and the plans for all that he had by the Spirit, of the courts of the house of the LORD....*   (1 Chronicles 28:11–12)

In 2 Chronicles, we see the results of Solomon's obedience to follow the pattern.

> *And the Levites who were the singers, all those of Asaph and Heman and Jeduthun, with their sons and their brethren, stood at the east end of the altar, clothed in white linen, having cymbals, stringed instruments*

and harps, and with them one hundred and twenty priests sounding with trumpets; indeed it came to pass, when the trumpeters and singers were as one, to make one sound to be heard in praising and thanking the Lord, *and when they lifted up their voice with the trumpets and cymbals and instruments of music, and praised the* Lord, *saying: "For He is good, for His mercy endures forever," that the house, the house of the* Lord, *was filled with a cloud, so that the priests could not continue ministering because of the cloud; for the glory of the* Lord *filled the house of God.* (2 Chronicles 5:12–14)

Every leader who followed the plan that David had received from the Lord possessed promises and prospered. The Word of God gives accounts of seven leaders who followed this pattern of the tabernacle of David. Two of these leaders were Nehemiah and Hezekiah.

Nehemiah rebuilt the walls by building as David did. (See Nehemiah 11–12.) About Hezekiah, we read,

And he did what was right in the sight of the Lord, *according to all that his father David had done. In the first year of his reign, in the first month, he opened the doors of the house of the* Lord *and repaired them. Then he brought in the priests and the Levites, and gathered them in the East Square, and said to them: "Hear me, Levites! Now sanctify yourselves, sanctify the house of the* Lord *God of your fathers, and carry out the rubbish from the holy place."* (2 Chronicles 29:2–5)

Jesus echoed the prophet Isaiah in calling the tabernacle of David a *"house of prayer"* (Matthew 21:13; see also Isaiah 56:7). The apostle John revealed the beauty of the tabernacle of David in Revelation 4–5. And in Acts 13:2, we see the priestly principle of ministering to God as was practiced in the tabernacle of David. In this passage, leaders ministered to God, and, as a result, the apostles Paul and Barnabas were sent forth to change the world. We find that once the tabernacle of David was rebuilt, God's glory overtook cities and nations. As this happens in the church today, we will reap the greatest harvest of souls that this world has ever known.

Praise Builds a Habitation for the Lord

The only way for us to rebuild the tabernacle of David is to create a habitation in which God can dwell. We do so through intense, corporate praise and worship and through united, fervent intercessory prayer. This requires pure and sincere hearts of the men and women who will set their eyes on the Lord.

It is our vision to establish a center in the Orlando area where we can employ teams of psalmists, musicians, and dancers to cover eight three-hour shifts each day. We began the realization of this mission by establishing Heart of David School of Worship, where we hold monthly meetings with the aim of restoring a passion for ministering to God through prayer, praise, and worship. We also travel across the country and overseas to assist other leaders in establishing centers like ours in their cities and nations.

What will we possess by rebuilding the tabernacle of David?

"On that day I will raise up the tabernacle of David, which has fallen down, and repair its damages; I will raise up its ruins, and rebuild it as in the days of old; that they may possess the remnant of Edom, and all the Gentiles who are called by My name," says the LORD *who does this thing. "Behold, the days are coming," says the* LORD, *"when the plowman shall overtake the reaper, and the treader of grapes him who sows seed; the mountains shall drip with sweet wine, and all the hills shall flow with it. I will bring back the captives of My people Israel; they shall build the waste cities and inhabit them; they shall plant vineyards and drink wine from them; they shall also make gardens and eat fruit from them. I will plant them in their land, and no longer shall they be pulled up from the land I have given them," says the* LORD *your God.* (Amos 9:11–15)

Here are just five of the many blessings we receive when we position ourselves to possess by rebuilding the tabernacle of David:

1. We will possess the harvest! (souls, souls, souls)

2. We will possess new wine! (refreshing, renewal, and revival)

3. We will possess, rebuild, and inhabit cities! (transformation of cities)

4. We will possess provision! (and the devil won't be able to steal it)

5. We will possess the land! (forever, never to be evicted)

Are you ready to possess the harvest? Are you thirsty for the new wine of the Holy Spirit? Would you like to be a part of transforming your city? Does living in the land of "more than enough" sound good? Are you tired of being a wilderness-walker? If so, trade in your sandals for mountain boots and arise as a promise-possessor today. Let's arise with a Davidic anointing, as Nehemiah and Hezekiah did, wielding the sword of praise with one hand and the trowel of prayer with the other. Together, we will rebuild the walls of the tabernacle of David and possess the land!

Your Part in the Building Process

Rebuilding the tabernacle of David is not just a lofty idea for the corporate body of Christ; it is for you personally, as you walk through your life and ministry.

What should you do when you've done all you can do and nothing is happening?

What should you do when life throws you a really bad deal?

What should you do when things are going so fast and furious that you have to stop and think a minute to remember your name? Build God a habitation through praise!

Lift up your hands and praise Him, even when it doesn't look good. When it doesn't look right or feel right, and you don't see anything happening, praise Him anyway. If you fill your mouth with praise and let the fruit of your lips bring thanksgiving and honor unto the name of Jesus—no matter what you're going through—you'll get access to places and people, you'll see an acceleration of the promises of God, and you'll see abundance flow in so that you can fulfill your destiny. Blessings that have been held up will be released. Blessings that have been delayed will be demonstrated before your eyes. Why? Because you have gone to war in the heavenlies by praising and worshipping God.

9

UNLEASHING THE POWER OF PRAISE

Judah also will fight at Jerusalem. And the wealth of all the surrounding nations shall be gathered together: gold, silver, and apparel in great abundance. (Zechariah 14:14)

As we've discussed, *Judah* means "praise." Genuine praise will fight. I'm talking about battle-cry praise—praise that wages war. Not wimpy praise, where you're thinking of all the other things you could be doing. I'm talking about focused, intense, passionate praise. The only way you're going to see breakthrough is by praising God with all your heart, mind, soul, and strength.

When you throw your entire being into praise, your hands become weapons. The Bible says that the Lord teaches our hands to war, to fight. (See Psalm 144:1.) When you clap your hands as praise to God, you're smiting the enemy. When you pick up your feet and begin to dance in praise to the Lord, you're putting the devil under your feet. You're making the enemy your footstool.

In the boxing ring, the one who lifts his hands at the end of the fight is the winner. The boxer who jumps up and down with his hands in the air is the victor. When you praise and worship God in the midst of your battle, you become *more* than a conqueror. (See Romans 8:37.)

Jesus is the conqueror because He kicked out the door of the tomb and rose triumphantly. That makes you and me more than conquerors every time we lift our hands, especially when we're tired and scared and need a miracle! At those times, we say, "No matter what the odds, we're more than conquerors because of Jesus Christ!"

Maybe you lift your hands in praise only when you receive something good. It's great to praise and thank God when you get something good. But what if you need something? If you need something, lift up your hands and give Jesus praise. If you'll give Him praise, then you're going to see your enemies flee and your God arise.

Let God Arise

Let God arise, let his enemies be scattered. (Psalm 68:1)

How does God arise?

He arises through the praises of His people. When we lift Him up, He rises in our midst and puts our enemies to flight. He sets an ambush for our enemies.

When you begin to praise God, you lift a two-edged sword. Your voice of praise to God pierces the heavens, where your blessings cannot be held back any longer. Why? Because your hands are up, your voice is lifted, your feet are dancing, you're praising God, and the devil is fleeing. When the enemy comes in one way, the Bible says he's got to flee seven ways. (See Deuteronomy 28:7.) He's beside himself! He can't even find himself when he leaves you!

Govern Your Soul

The only way to govern the heavenlies and possess territories for the Lord is to first govern your own soul. You must take charge of your mind, will, and emotions through the power of the Holy Spirit.

I call this "soul control." If you don't control your soul, it will control you. Remember that you are a spirit that possesses a soul that lives in a body. Keep that in order, and you'll conquer new territory, every day. Self-government will increase spiritual authority to reign and rule in life. As you govern your soul, you will soar higher in prophetic praise. When you begin subjecting your feelings and emotions to God's Word, you'll see greater results than you've ever seen before.

If you've never done this, at first, when you praise God and you don't feel like it, your mind's going to say, *You're crazy. You're a hypocrite. You don't feel any of this.*

You need to respond by saying, "No, I don't walk by feelings. I don't walk by sight. I walk by faith, and I'm going to praise Him anyway!"

Maybe you're thinking, *Well, if the Lord will do this miracle, then I'll praise Him.*

But the Lord says, in effect, "You praise Me first, and then I'll do it."

What do you think a sacrifice of praise is, anyway? A *sacrifice* is something you do, even if you don't necessarily feel like doing it. Your body hurts, your heart aches, someone just got on your last nerve—but you're going to praise God anyway. That's a sacrifice.

Anybody can praise God when he feels good. Anybody can praise God when everything's going all right—and we should. "Praise God, I have money in the bank. Praise God, I'm getting married. Praise God, I got a promotion." But what about the times when you don't have a job? What about those times when you don't have a place to live? What about those times when you don't have a friend who'll listen? Are you going to praise Him then?

Everybody's mad at you. Nobody likes you. Your family is rejecting you, but you say, "God, I thank You that I've got a family in heaven. I'm in Your family right here on earth. I've got Jesus in my heart, my Father's on the throne, and the Holy Spirit is helping me. He's my Comforter and Friend."

The enemy tries you because you start pressing through on God's Word. When you begin meeting some resistance, your mind says, *Hey, I didn't have all this hell when I wasn't fighting. I didn't have all this trouble when I wasn't trying to do anything for God. As long as I peacefully coexisted with the devil and compromised with everybody, everything was going all right. I'm going to go back to the way it used to be.*

Remember the way it used to be? You weren't happy. You weren't fulfilling your destiny. You were taking up space, sucking air, and going nowhere. But now you're fighting, you're pursuing, you're moving—and you're facing some resistance. Being at the point of resistance is not the place to stop!

Praise Your Way Through the Pain

If you press through when you don't feel like it—if you give God praise when circumstances aren't going right—things will begin to turn around. I know you're going through situations and facing tough times where you need a breakthrough. The only way to break through is to praise your way through it. It's not going to happen if you talk about it. It's not going to happen if you wish it. It's not going to happen if you think about it. You're going to have to open up your mouth and praise the King of Kings. Lift up your hands, shout, stomp, and dance!

10

BRINGING HEAVEN TO EARTH

For though we walk in the flesh, we do not war according to the flesh.
For the weapons of our warfare are not carnal but mighty in God for
pulling down strongholds. (2 Corinthians 10:3–4)

This passage is a picture of apostolic prayer, prayer that wars against the powers of darkness so that the veil of blindness over people, cities, and nations is removed, and the truth of the gospel can be released and received.

I'm going to declare something about the times in which we are living. I believe the church has not hit her knees like this since the first century. I believe we are in an hour when prayer is going to bring heaven to earth and sweep nations into the kingdom of God.

Why do I say this? Because believers are really seeking the mind and heart of the Father. We're hearing about the things that He wants to see happen on the earth, and we're not praying little "Please, God, please, if it be Thy will" prayers. Instead, we're coming out of our prayer closets and showing up at prayer meetings to tear down the strongholds of the enemy and release the prophetic word of the Lord into the earth.

> *Ask of Me, and I will give You the nations for Your inheritance, and the very ends of the earth as Your possession.* (Psalm 2:8 NASB)

Apostolic prayer asks for nations, because that's what God desires. God is raising up "Hannah houses" that are birthing a "Samuel generation"! You'll see what I mean in a moment.

You serve a big God who loves to grant big requests. He desires for you to ask Him for the big things. He is raising up prayer warriors like Hannah in this hour. They will not let go of the horns of the altar until they see God's will done on earth as it is in heaven. Hannah's destiny was to be fruitful and multiply according to God's Word, and she refused to budge until she saw His word manifested in her life.

> *So Hannah rose up after they had eaten in Shiloh, and after they had drunk. Now Eli the priest sat upon a seat by a post of the temple of the LORD. And she was in bitterness of soul, and prayed unto the LORD, and wept sore. And she vowed a vow, and said, O LORD of hosts, if thou wilt indeed look on the affliction of thine handmaid, and remember me, and not forget thine handmaid, but wilt give unto thine handmaid a man child, then I will give him unto the LORD all the days of his life, and there shall no razor come upon his head. And it came to pass, as she continued praying before the LORD, that Eli marked her mouth.* (1 Samuel 1:9–12 KJV)

This is what is happening in the church right now. There is a company of intercessors, a people of warfare, who are praying unlike they've ever prayed before. They're entering into new realms of spiritual warfare, and many of the religious and traditional folk do not understand what they are doing. Like Eli, they are marking the mouths of those who are prayer warriors. But we must keep praying, for out of our spirits, our prayers will give birth to a Samuel generation, the likes of which this world has never known!

> *And Eli said unto her, How long wilt thou be drunken? put away thy wine from thee. And Hannah answered and said, No, my lord, I am a woman of a sorrowful spirit: I have drunk neither wine nor strong drink, but have poured out my soul before the LORD. Count not thine handmaid for a daughter of Belial: for out of the abundance of my complaint and grief have I spoken hitherto. Then Eli answered and said, Go in peace: and the God of Israel grant thee thy petition that thou hast asked of him.* (1 Samuel 1:14–17 KJV)

Hannah continued in prayer, even though the religious order marked her and accused her of being drunk. We must have this same excellent spirit if we are going to rise up higher. God honored Hannah's faith, perseverance, and courage. Access was granted, and the great prophet Samuel was born to her.

In the process of praying to obtain the promise, Hannah rose up higher!

> *And she said, Let thine handmaid find grace in thy sight. So the woman went her way, and did eat, and her countenance was no more sad.* (1 Samuel 1:18 KJV)

When God grants you access to go higher, you've got to remove the sackcloth and ashes and praise Him. Worship the Lord because of His promise!

> *And they rose up in the morning early, and worshipped before the LORD, and returned, and came to their house to Ramah: and Elkanah knew Hannah his wife; and the LORD remembered her. Wherefore it came to pass, when the time was come about after Hannah had conceived, that she bare a son, and called his name Samuel, saying, Because I have asked him of the LORD.* (1 Samuel 1:19–20 KJV)

All of this happened because Hannah prayed. She asked the Lord for a son, and her prayers gave birth to the prophet Samuel, who had an anointing to shift the heavens.

Shifting the Heavens

Your prayers will shift the heavens, too.

God is raising up Hannahs who will give birth to Samuels! I see entire congregations being transformed by the power of the Spirit into "Hannah houses." These Hannah houses will give birth to the greatest prophetic generation this world has ever known. I hear the Lord say, "Hannah, Hannah, come forth and give birth to My Samuels." Can you hear Him calling? "Hannah, Hannah, come forth!" I hear the Lord saying, "Samuel, Samuel. Yes, a generation of Samuels is arising."

Samuels are *shifters!* They are a "shift generation," and wherever they go, they shift atmospheres. Whatever they prophesy comes to pass.

Samuel prophesied, and not even one word failed to make an impact. Samuel shifted the priesthood and shifted governments. He prophesied the end of the priestly service of Eli and his son. Samuel prophesied the end of Saul's reign and the beginning of David's rule. So it is with the generation of Samuels that's arising today. These "Samuel shifters" are shifting administrations within both the church and civil government.

I hear the Spirit of the Lord saying, *Shift!* God is shifting gears, and we must shift with Him. This shift will take us to the next level. There is a shift that we must embrace in order to reap the last harvest.

This is not just a generational shift; it is something we must discern in our everyday lives in order for us to cross over and possess our Promised Land. Many leaders have been stuck, and, like a gear that is positioned improperly, they will burn out if they refuse to make the shifts God requires of them.

Those who will shift in accordance with God's leading will be exalted and will eat the good fruit of the land. It is time for us to shift in the following ways:

- *Shift in leadership*—from Elis to Samuels, from Sauls to Davids. (See 2 Samuel 1:5, 9–10, 13, 15, 17.) Samuels, Davids, and Joshuas are coming forth to lead the shift generation—the anchor generation.

- *Shift of paradigm*—from sheep to soldiers; from lambs to lions.

- *Shift of focus*—from the local church to the kingdom of God.

- *Shift to the today dimension*—(See Ezra 5:1–2, 6:14–15; John 2:1–11, 19–21; Hosea 6:1–3, Joshua 3.)

- *Shift in wealth*—wealth will begin to shift into the hands of the righteous.

- *Shift in structure*—from man's order to God's order. (See 1 Samuel 6; Ephesians 2:20–22.)

- *Shift from shame to fame*—(See Zephaniah 3:19–20.)

- *Shift in geography*—there will be greater movement and even the relocating of ministries, as God rearranges seats of leadership for those who remain faithful and teachable.

- *Shift in the heavenlies*—God is releasing fresh anointing and additional angelic forces into the earth.

- *Shift in church membership*—an exodus has begun as saints flee from dead, religious churches to churches where the life of the Spirit flows more freely and the Word of God is truly lived out. The churches that are shifting with God's apostolic restoration are seeing exponential growth. Others are decreasing because they are resisting the moves of God or they are refusing to restrain spiritual children who are living in sin.

Changing of the Guard

While ministering in Taiwan in 1997, I had the privilege of witnessing a clear illustration of a shift that captivated me. It was the changing of the guard at the National Chiang Kai-shek Memorial Hall. Chiang Kai-shek, the founding president of Taiwan, was also a Christian. As I watched the changing of the guard, the Lord revealed some things that I had never seen while watching the changing of the guard in other countries.

A statue of President Chiang Kai-shek stood in the center of the main room of the memorial. Approximately seventy-five feet on either side of the statue was a soldier standing guard on top of a pedestal that looked to be about two feet in height. I watched in amazement as these two soldiers stood with their guns outstretched, facing the memorial and each other, without moving a muscle.

As changing time arrived, I could hear soldiers marching in unison in the distance. Those around me were saying, "They're coming! They're coming!" Everyone watched the hallway in anticipation of their arrival. I did not know until later that the distinct sound that had captivated my attention was coming from metal taps on the bottom of the soldiers' boots.

After hearing those sounds but not seeing anything for quite a while, three soldiers rounded the corner. The leading soldier had a scroll of orders beneath his arm, and the two soldiers marching behind him had bayonets resting upon their shoulders. When they all came to a stop, the two soldiers who were standing guard simultaneously hit their guns on their pedestals and dismounted. They left their posts, marching in unison: *tap, step, tap, step, tap, step.* They were at least one hundred fifty feet apart at the beginning, yet they stayed in sync and moved as one!

Marching to the center, these two soldiers joined ranks with the other three and faced the memorial with their backs to us. Suddenly they turned, facing each other. At the command of the soldier in the middle— the one with the scroll—they hit their guns on the ground and tilted them toward each other, saluting. Then, almost faster than you could blink, they changed places. They hit their guns on the floor and then tilted them forward again.

The soldiers who had the next watch marched to the pedestals and took their posts. They hit their guns on their pedestals and tilted them toward each other. I watched as the former guards marched out of the room. On the right shoulder of each of their uniforms was a woven patch depicting a roaring lion.

This experience had a profound impact on me. Here are some insights I had as I witnessed the changing of the guard:

+ When we are on guard, we are to be sober and vigilant.

+ When it's time to *shift*, whether coming on duty or going off, we move the moment the clock strikes.

+ Unity creates a distinct sound, and we must march together in rank and order. (See Joel 2–3; Psalm 133; Ephesians 4.)

+ The five soldiers represent the fivefold ministry gifts. (See Ephesians 4:11.)

+ The soldier who had the scroll beneath his arm represents the apostle. Apostles are graced to establish governments, which cause divine order within the body of Christ. When operating correctly, an apostle discerns which fivefold ministry's anointing is needed for a particular situation or portion of a service, and he releases people to function in their callings and gifts.

+ The other four soldiers represent the prophet, evangelist, pastor, and teacher. These four remain vigilant so that they can take their *shift* when called upon. While not on a pedestal, they are to support those who are with prayer and prepare for their next *shift* (clean and load their guns—in other words, study, fast, and pray).

+ Shifts come more often than we think. If we're not ready, one of two things may happen:

  1. Those on post will stay on post too long and burn out or fall asleep on duty, which creates an opening for the enemy to come in.

  2. Those who are ready and willing to take their *shift* are unable to fulfill their destinies. This can cause soldiers to become disheartened and disillusioned.

+ The patch with the roaring lion represents the fact that we are being transformed from sheep into soldiers, from lambs into lions. We are authorized to enforce the dominion of the Lion of Judah.

+ When the soldiers tilted their swords toward each other, they were preferring one another, releasing and empowering one another to take their *shift*.

When you begin to pray from the innermost part of your being to birth God's will into the earth as a shift, it will be a prayer of groaning and a place of travail. You are giving birth to what God wants—the nations.

Apostolic prayer brings God's order as well as His orders. Apostolic prayer brings the strategies of God to defeat the enemy. Apostolic prayer brings the world to the Lord Jesus Christ!

So Samuel grew, and the LORD was with him and let none of his words fall to the ground. (1 Samuel 3:19)

Why did none of Samuel's words fall to the ground? Samuel had learned from his mother how to pray and minister to the Lord. He spoke only what God told him to speak. He decreed the word of the King, and it was so.

And Elisha said to [the king], "Take a bow and some arrows." So he took himself a bow and some arrows. Then he said to the king of Israel, "Put your hand on the bow." So he put his hand on it, and Elisha put his hands on the king's hands. (2 Kings 13:15–16)

I believe that nations are shifting because God's prayer warriors are rising up in praise, prayer, and prophecy. We are placing our hands upon government officials and receiving divine strategies to effect lasting change in the world.

Engaging in prophetic praise is not a profession or event; it's a lifestyle. It is a journey that will never end—until you stand before God's glorious throne at the end of your earthly life and begin your unending praise of Him, face-to-face.

Psalm 24:6 states, "*This is Jacob, the generation of those who seek Him, who seek Your face.*" Are you part of this generation of Jacob? Do you want proceeding praise to overflow from your life, blessing all those around you, as well as the rest of the world? This is a critical hour on planet Earth. We are the generation preparing for the return of the Lord Jesus Christ. This is the *kairos* season—and we are a generation that is determined to seek God's face, to know Him intimately, and to govern as He would have us to rule and reign upon this earth. We have had the baby boomer generation; we've had the Generation-Xers. Now it's time for the prophetic praisers!

11

DOWNLOAD HEAVEN

One Hebrew word for "worship" is *shachah*, which means "to bow down, to prostrate oneself." When I *shachah*, I receive a download from heaven. If I want a download, I have to get down low. When I humble myself, God will exalt me.

My Download Is Found in My "Down Low"!

When I worship, I am subjecting myself to a higher force. When I am uploading praise, I am transmitting a signal from a smaller computer to a higher source that can contain it. You see, God can contain all of the worship in the earth. In fact, there is not enough worship coming from earth right now. If there was more worship, God could contain it easily. His hard drive, or "heart"-drive, is so open to receiving worship that we can upload and transmit worship from our "heart"-drive directly to His. When I transmit that signal to him, I am down-"lowing"—getting to a place where I am down low—and I am saying, "You are supreme, higher, and greater. I need to upload to You, because You are the only One who can contain this, the only One who is worthy of this." When I upload praise to God, that same signal strength or currency of worship comes back down as rain with whatever I need. It also comes down as *reign*. I can reign in whatever arena I find myself.

One of the Greek words for "worship" is *proskyneo*, meaning "to kiss the hand toward one, in token of reverence." It is to kneel or lay prostrate and to pay homage to someone.

When I kneel or bow down, there is an upload. When you go before the King, you always bow. In most Asian cultures, humility is prized. Gestures of respect are of utmost importance. It seems this has been somewhat lost in the culture of America. So many people want to do what they want to do, when they want to do it. If a person is lawless and rebellious, it will rob him of the download of heaven. If a person cannot bow before the Lord and cannot submit to His Word and His delegated authority in his life, he will not see an upload. Will you worship the Lord? Will you love Him? Tell Him, "I love You, I worship You, I honor You! You are my Daddy, my Friend, my Majesty, my King, the Lover of my soul. I worship You!"

Many people have lost their ability to "get low" in the church. Many people are getting their heads cut off in spiritual warfare. Do you know why so many people are getting blown to bits in this war for the kingdom? It is because their heads are lifted up in pride. In war, you must stay low. You don't walk tall, asking to be shot. You think about the bullets flying, and you get down. Why are you getting low? Because you don't want to get your head blown off! We have too many believers and leaders with big heads. Yet we don't see Jesus like that. He got down on His knees and washed the disciples' feet. (See John 13:3–15.) Jesus got low! And because Jesus got down low, there is a download from heaven, today. God is looking for soldiers who will get down so low that the enemy will not be able to take their heads off.

The D.O.W.N.L.O.A.D.

D = Drink

As the deer pants for the water brooks, so pants my soul for You, O God. (Psalm 42:1)

If I want a download, I must learn to drink up His presence. When I go to a water fountain, I can stand in front of it and smile, but water won't bubble up for me to drink. I can wave my hand over it and stomp my foot, but still it won't provide water. In order to drink from the water, I must press the button. There are a lot of people who want a download from heaven but they don't know how to "push the button." There is a button that releases a download. That button is *worship*!

How lovely is Your tabernacle, O Lord of hosts! My soul longs, yes, even faints for the courts of the Lord; my heart and my flesh cry out for the living God. (Psalm 84:1–2)

If you are thirsty enough, you will do anything to get the download. If you just say, "Well, I think I'll have a little sip of water," you are not ready! Don't think—drink! Drink His presence. People who are full of religion, full of themselves, full of pride, and full of everything in this world will sit in church, yet it won't do anything for them. They wake up on Monday with no thought of pursuing God. They wake up on Tuesday and find that it's more important to get on the Internet than it is to get with God. They wake up on Wednesday, Thursday, and Friday, and it's more of the same. Everything around them is more important! But, when you find someone who is really thirsty, it is as the psalmist wrote: *"As the deer pants for the water brooks, so pants my soul for You, O God."* Someone who truly thirsts for God will run after Him, like a man in the desert, looking off in the distance, seeing water, running, falling on his face, falling on his knees, and trying everything he can think of to get to that place where he can get just one drink. Are you that thirsty?

O = Oil

Behold, how good and how pleasant it is for brethren to dwell together in unity! It is like the precious oil upon the head, running down on the beard, the beard of Aaron, running down on the edge of his garments. It is like the dew of Hermon, descending upon the mountains of Zion; for there the LORD commanded the blessing—life forevermore.

(Psalm 133:1–3)

The oil flows down. If we want to live beneath the download of heaven, of glory, and of blessing, we have to live in a life that is submitted to authority. Many people don't like the word *submit*, but we can't move forward if we don't come under authority. Submission is literally coming under the mission. At Legacy Life Church, we have a vision—a mission that God has given us. The mission of Legacy Life is to "awaken generations." That is our mission as believers, and as a house. Everything we do must come into alignment with that mission. If someone wants to be a part of that mission, he must come under it and submit to it. Like a submarine, he goes down and comes under that mission. You can't get to the oil unless you become a part of the garments of the house. It's like *"the dew...upon the mountains of Zion."* You have to be on the mountain to receive the dew that comes down from the top. When snow hits the mountain, where does it hit first? On top, and then it melts and flows down. It releases the water for anyone on that mountain. The streams that flow from that mountain are replenished from the heavens. Likewise, the oil flows downward.

Let me break it down a little further. If I have a job and I want to be blessed in it, I have to submit to the authority over it. I can't just show up to work and expect to receive a paycheck unless I accomplish the things that my superior wants me to accomplish. I can't be working against my manager's purposes and doing my own thing. I must "come under" that employer and the vision for that "house." I shouldn't merely be working for a paycheck; I should want to see that business succeed and be blessed. I should come as Joseph approached his position in the palace, knowing that God has anointed me, and that because I am in this position, my company will prosper. I won't go against this company; I will come under the visionary of the company and see to it that I do whatever I can, to the best of my ability, to further that company. If I can further that business, then, instead of just getting a forty-hour paycheck at the end of the week, I will prosper as that business prospers. I submit; I come under. You cannot expect to be blessed if you show up late, leave early, and take time off when you should be working. You can't spend your time talking to others, surfing the Internet, and doing your nails when you should be working. You can't expect to be blessed when you are stealing from your employer. You are robbing those who are in a position of authority over you, and God will not bless a thief.

When I come under the authority of someone who is over me, and I realize that I am not just abiding by the rules for a paycheck but am working to further the vision of my employer, then God will give me what belongs to me, because I have been faithful over something that belongs to someone else. If I am faithful over another person's vineyard, God will reward me with a vineyard of my own. How does a business owner acquire his own business? At some point in his life, more than likely, he had to work a minimum-wage job, being faithful to the business of another man. That is how God honored him.

The principle is this: There is authority in the household—namely, the parents. In every house, there is a mission and a vision. As a child of God, you are an employee of Father and Son, Incorporated, or Mama and Kids, Incorporated. As an employee in the family business, you have to come under it and walk in accordance with what God has for that house, in order to live in the blessings of that house. When you step out from under authority and challenge it, or when you refuse to submit to authority, then you live under a curse. Now, the curse won't affect the family, because they are walking in alignment. Whoever is in order will receive the blessing, but whoever subverts authority waives his right to the blessing. If you want to receive the blessing, you have to come under the daddy, the mama, or the authority in the house. You must submit.

If you want to live in the penthouse, you must first learn how to live in the basement. The Bible says, *"Whoever exalts himself will be humbled, and he who humbles himself will be exalted"* (Matthew 23:12).

It doesn't matter your age. If you lease out a room in someone's house, you are under that person's authority. If you must submit to that authority, you will walk in alignment and blessing. When you come under authority, blessing flows. When you are under the covering of favor, under the covering of provision, you are blessed. God is obligated to bless you. When you refuse to submit, it isn't that God removes the blessing; it's more the case that you walk out from under the covering of that blessing.

If I worked for a carpet-cleaning business and took advantage of the company by driving around, running personal errands, and wasting the company's gasoline, what would you think? Instead of getting my assigned job done and making money for the company, what did I do? I came out from under my authority and walked into a curse. Not only am I, myself, losing money, but I am also losing money for the company. Eventually, the company would have to let me go. I could have kept my job and advanced the business if I would have cleaned carpet, as I was supposed to. They would still have more work for me, but instead, I wasted their gas and their time.

It doesn't matter how old you are; if you are in the house, you are under authority. You may think, *Well, I'm old enough to vote now, and I'm old enough to join the military.* Let me tell you something: please join the military, because then you'll find out what it means to have no say in what you wear, how you do your hair, what time you wake up, or what you eat. You won't even decide when to go to the bathroom!

Some people say, "God has removed the blessing," when what really happened is, they came out from under the authority—specifically, by failing to tithe.

Will a man rob God? Yet you have robbed Me! But you say, "In what way have we robbed You?" In tithes and offerings. (Malachi 3:8)

You didn't just show up in God's house and take His money while He was gone. You held Him at gunpoint; you held Him up. When you withhold your tithe, you're robbing God, and you come out from under His blessing and favor. Now you won't be able to get heaven's download. The download is available only when you are in alignment.

There is a download when you are under kingdom authority. God is obligated by His Word. He will not bless you if you are out from under His authority. You may think, *Well, why are some people in the world blessed?* You have to understand that someone might be working secularly to get earthly gain. The Bible tells you to consider the end of his way—he might be getting it all right now, but in the end, it comes down to Proverbs 14:12: *"There is a way that seems right to a man, but its end is the way of death."*

All that money won't pay for good health; all that money won't pay for peace of mind; all that money and stuff he thinks he's worked for did not come from living for God. All those things will pass away. The Bible says, *"To him who knows to do good and does not do it, to him it is sin"* (James 4:17). You know that you have to be under the covering, because going out from under it is sin. Stay beneath the download.

Regardless of age, if children want to live a blessed life, and if they are still living at home, they need to do what they can to serve the visionary of your house. Serve your dad; serve your mom; walk in alignment with order, and the blessing will flow down. Watch what will happen! You will walk out and possess your own land, your own house; you will have your own job and your own blessing—not because you did it by yourself but because the Bible says that if you honor your parents, you will have long life. (See Exodus 20:12.) You will be thankful for your parents and the blessing they are to you. When you go out and receive your blessing, you will turn around and bless them in return.

In Jewish culture, when the oldest son comes of age, everything the parents have is bestowed upon him. You know what happens then? His parents become his responsibility. He says, "You provided covering for me, so now I will take care of you." That is honor. That is coming under authority.

There have been seasons when I have watched my dad take care of his father and mother. He gave them food and covered their car and house payments. You know why? Because they took care of him when he had nothing. They brought him into the world, they honored him, and now, he is looking out for them in return. That is honorable, and God will remember and reward him for that.

W = Work the Word

You can't expect to have the download if you don't work the Word of God and the prophetic words God gives to you. If He gives you a prophetic word, be a "doer" of it. Faith without action is dead. (See James 2:17.) Every time you see a Nike swoosh, you should hear the voice of God, saying, "Just do it!" God is trying to capture our attention through things like this, even through secular songs like Janet Jackson's "What Have You Done for Me Lately?" Can you hear the angels singing that old Elvis song, "A Little Less Talk and a Lot More Action"? You've got to work the Word! If you will work the Word, the Word will work for you!

> *For if anyone is a hearer of the word and not a doer, he is like a man observing his natural face in a mirror; for he observes himself, goes away, and immediately forgets what kind of man he was.*
> (James 1:23–24)

> *But do you want to know, O foolish man, that faith without works is dead?* (James 2:20)

> *This charge I commit to you, son Timothy, according to the prophecies previously made concerning you, that by them you may wage the good warfare.* (1 Timothy 1:18)

Warfare with the Word! Nowhere in the Bible will you find it telling you to put the Word on a shelf. It's time to take the written Word and the *rhema* (God-uttered or prophetic) word concerning your life off of the shelf, dust them off, and go to war with them. If God has given you a promise from His Word, or a prophetic word that aligns with His Word, then you must begin to wield it as a weapon! Use God's Word as a sword or a ramming rod, and boldly declare, "God has said (fill in the blank) concerning my life, and I decree that it will come to pass!" Then, begin releasing the sounds of prophetic praise, expecting the download of heaven in your life!

N = "Now" Faith

Now faith is the substance of things hoped for, the evidence of things not seen. (Hebrews 11:1)

You have to have "now" faith! "If it's not *now*, it's not faith." Those were the words the Lord spoke to my dad the night he was raised out of a wheelchair. You see, my father was in an airplane crash and was lost for more than fifteen hours in the wreckage of the plane. All night long, he was lying in gasoline, nearly drowning in his own blood. His nose was cut off, his knee was ripped off, his hip was broken to pieces, and his left foot was torn off, except for the heel cord. He sustained numerous other injuries—by all accounts, he should have died—*but for God.*

When he would feel death coming, he would quote Psalm 118:17: *"I shall not die, but live, and declare the works of the Lord."* When a flight surgeon finally arrived at my dad's side, he predicted that Dad wouldn't make it to the hospital, because he had lost too much blood. Dad said, "I shall not die!" After numerous surgeries and more than six weeks in the hospital, Dad was released to go home. Eight doctors and specialists told him that he would never stand or walk again. However, at a midweek church service, Dad was preaching on the subject of faith from his wheelchair when he heard the Lord say, "Charlie Fowler, if it's not *now*, it's not faith!" Dad asked for everyone who believed that he would walk that night to stand and start praising the Lord. Now that's prophetic praise—to start praising before you see anything happen! As people began to praise the Lord, Dad began quoting Isaiah 53:5: *"By His stripes we are healed."* Then, he said, "So, if we are, and we were, then I am healed!" With that, he stood up and started walking. The place went crazy and erupted in praise! The next day, he went to see those same doctors who had told him that he would never walk, and they said it was a miracle! My dad is still walking, running, and preaching today. He and my mom pastor a church in northern Florida and continue to see "now faith" work in many lives!

L = Loaded

Blessed be the Lord, who daily loads us with benefits, the God of our salvation! (Psalm 68:19)

Live the "loaded life," one that is daily loaded with benefits. Don't live beneath God's standard for your life. Expect God's best and don't settle for anything less. When you join this prophetic praise army, your life will be a living testimony of what happens when heaven is downloaded! Your family, friends, neighbors, and coworkers will begin to ask, "What are you doing?" When this happens, remember to give God the glory; then, enlist them as a disciple of worship.

Bless the LORD, O my soul, and forget not all His benefits. (Psalm 103:2)

What shall I render to the LORD for all His benefits toward me? (Psalm 116:12)

O = Obedience

In order to download heaven on earth, we must be obedient to God's voice. To tap into the supernatural realm of God requires sensitive vessels who are quick to obey His gentle nudges. We can't be stubborn or hardheaded. We must be pliable in the hands of the Potter. Swift obedience releases high-speed downloads of heaven on earth.

I'm reminded of Naaman. Seven times, the prophet told him to dip in the Jordan River. What would have happened if Naaman had not obeyed? Absolutely nothing, other than that death would have quickly taken him. However, because he obeyed, he was not only healed but also made whole.

So he went down and dipped seven times in the Jordan, according to the saying of the man of God; and his flesh was restored like the flesh of a little child, and he was clean. (2 Kings 5:14)

How many are struggling with sicknesses or circumstances that aren't necessary? All God is waiting for is their obedience. One act of obedience could change your life forever. Who is it that God told you to share His love with? Whom did He tell you to bless? What ministry did He lay on your heart to sow a seed into? Whatever the act of obedience, do it now. Don't delay, for delayed obedience is disobedience, and disobedience is witchcraft. (See 1 Samuel 15:23.) Stop trying to conjure things up in your flesh. Get in the spirit and obey. Then you'll see heaven manifested on earth.

To obey is better than sacrifice...for rebellion is as the sin of witch-craft. (1 Samuel 15:22–23)

"If you are willing and obedient, you shall eat the good of the land; but if you refuse and rebel, you shall be devoured by the sword"; for the mouth of the Lord has spoken. (Isaiah 1:19–20)

A = Agreement

Again I say to you that if two of you agree on earth concerning any-thing that they ask, it will be done for them by My Father in heaven. For where two or three are gathered together in My name, I am there in the midst of them. (Matthew 18:19–20)

If you want a download from heaven, you must live a life of agree-ment. I'm not saying that you must agree with everything you hear. The verses above state that if two or three agree about something in prayer,

God will perform it. The Bible also says, "*Can two walk together, unless they are agreed?*" (Amos 3:3). So, if somebody is living contrary to the vision for a house, business, church, or any other group of believers—if he is robbing from what your spouse, parents, boss, or church has built—how can you walk with that person unless he comes back into agreement? You cannot be yoked with someone who is contrary to the vision of your house or business. When I am in agreement, God will bless my life.

D = Discipleship

Go therefore and make disciples of all the nations, baptizing them in the name of the Father and of the Son and of the Holy Spirit.
(Matthew 28:19)

If I want to live in the download of heaven, I have to be under the authority of someone as a disciple, and I have to be willing to go and disciple someone else. What is a disciple? A disciple is one who is disciplined and committed to following the person who is discipling him. In order to be a disciple, I have to be disciplined, diligent, and under authority. Do you see the common thread? Oil flows down, and *download* ends with a "D," for *Discipleship*. How are we going to reach cities and nations? Discipleship. How will the kingdom of God advance? Discipleship. We must become disciples, or disciplined followers of Christ. We must become disciples of worship who are raising up disciples of worship. As we do this, we will cover the earth with His glory! Then we will govern territories and the heavenlies, and the greatest awakening this world has ever known will sweep over the nations, and the Lord will return for His bride.

One of the ways the Lord has instructed me to help disciple the nations is through Awake University and Awake School of Worship. For the last twenty-five-plus years, I have learned a lot by traveling worldwide, conducting Heart of David Worship Conferences and 24 Hours of Glory Gatherings. I've raised up anointed instructors and practitioners and have developed training modules that not only educate believers in the biblical, practical, and technical areas of prophetic praise, but also activate them into releasing deeper dimensions and demonstrations of the kingdom of God wherever they are sent. Some of those students have moved to Orlando, Florida, to become interns in a two-year training program. Others have taken online classes or come to monthly or annual activations. We also have IMPACT Sessions, in which people from all over the world come to Orlando for two weeks of intensive, concentrated training and activation. I also send teams to teach various modules of the Awake School of Worship in churches and conferences across the country and overseas.

Another way the Lord has instructed me to disciple the nations in uploading worship and downloading heaven through prophetic praise is through the GodDay mandate. On October 12, 2012 (12/12/12), thousands of believers from several cities, states, and nations gathered in the heart of Orlando to restore honor to God through united praise, prayer, and prophecy. For twelve hours, we showed forth the greatness of our God. We also demonstrated the Father's love by putting more than six thousand pairs of new shoes on the feet of fatherless children. The Lord originally gave me this idea in a vision in which I was lifted in the Spirit high above Orlando so that God could show me how the awakening that began with GodDay was going to travel around the world. In the vision, we walked from Orlando to New York City, and I watched as thousands worshipped and put shoes on the feet of fatherless children. Then, God took me to Australia, where I watched as thousands of people gathered in worship and put shoes on the feet of fatherless children. In the years to come, we will continue this mandate, with annual gatherings in Orlando, as well as in other cities and nations around the world. By His Spirit, together, we will "awaken cities to awaken nations." Through His anointing, we will restore honor to God and father the fatherless.

Calling All Believers to Become Prophetic Praisers!

Today, I love my Internet signal. Uploads and downloads are transmitted in a flash! Because of high-speed Internet connection, I no longer have to wait to upload or download files from my computer. So it is with the life of a believer who daily uploads prophetic praise and worship. Unfortunately, when you ask some believers what God is saying to them, they have to go away for forty days to fast and pray. Have you ever wondered why so many believers say, "Well, I'll pray about that"? I have. It's like they still have a weak dial-up connection. It's not high-speed. However, when you ask the same question of people who are uploading prophetic praise and worship, there is an immediate download. When you ask for prayer or a word from people who have a good upload signal, there is going to be a download, and God will speak. Why? Because they are uploading worship.

> *For as the rain comes down, and the snow from heaven, and do not return there, but water the earth, and make it bring forth and bud, that it may give seed to the sower and bread to the eater, so shall My word be that goes forth from My mouth; it shall not return to Me void, but it shall accomplish what I please, and it shall prosper in the thing for which I sent it.* (Isaiah 55:10–11)

You need to check your heavenly signal strength on a daily basis. Make sure your upload and download transmissions are flowing at the speed of heaven. Make sure you don't have anything obstructing your communication with the Lord. Report in frequently. Smith Wigglesworth said, "It's not how long you pray, it's how long you go without praying!" It was said of Wigglesworth that he would check in with God every hour that he was awake! Meet with your "circle of intensity" regularly to intensify and increase your passion for God. Stay in the flow continually, releasing the sounds of prophetic praise and receiving supernatural downloads of heaven that manifest as signs, wonders, and miracles wherever you go.

I see an army of worshippers arising around the world, uploading prophetic praise and downloading heaven on earth! Won't you help us impact the world for Christ? Won't you join our army of praisers and begin to download the kingdom of heaven on earth?

If you hear the clarion call to join this army, lift your hands and make this declaration:

I decree and declare that an army is arising with prophetic praise, uploading worship and downloading heaven on earth. I take my seat with Christ in heavenly places. I am no longer looking up at the enemy. I assume my delegated position and look down on the enemies of the kingdom of God. I sit with Christ and laugh the enemy into derision. As a governor, I wield praise as a weapon and execute the judgments of the Lord. I release the sounds of heaven, and in the name of Jesus, I tell the devil to shut up. No weapon formed against me shall prosper, and I pass sentence on every tongue that rises against me. (See Isaiah 54:17.)

Because the fire of God is burning in my life, I am too hot to handle and too bold to hold for the enemy. Jailhouses rock and prison doors open through my praise, and many captives are set free by the presence of the Lord. I penetrate through praise, prayer, and prophecy, and I'm saturated with His presence. As the rain of heaven, I cause God's glory to permeate the earth wherever I go. I have a destiny to reign and rule with Christ, to govern the heavenlies, and to subdue territories for the kingdom of God. As a member of the body of Christ and His holy congress, I pass divine legislation that thwarts the plans of darkness and releases the blessings and promises of the Lord. I render powerless the enemy's tactics of sickness, disease, division, doubt, lack, poverty, debt, divorce, depression, deception, accusation, curse, and anything that tries to rise up against my life, my family, and my church. I invoke the name that is above every name, the mighty and matchless name of Jesus, and I enforce the divine decree and promises of God's Word, which have been ratified by His shed blood! I appropriate the provisions, prosperity, and power of Christ's will in my life and territory. From this day forward, I will maintain a high-speed connection with God through prophetic praise. I will upload worship and download heaven wherever I go. In Jesus' name, amen.

ABOUT THE AUTHOR

Joshua Fowler is the Senior Leader of Legacy Life Church in Orlando, Florida. He has a rich heritage of ministry, with a great-grandfather who preached seventy years and grandfather who started two missions on a Navajo reservation. Since birth, Joshua has traveled throughout America, ministering with his parents. Joshua recently celebrated his twenty-fifth year of ministry. He is sought after as a conference speaker in the U.S. and abroad and has ministered extensively in many nations around the world. Joshua is the founder of GodDay, a movement dedicated to awakening cities and nations for God. He also founded Shoes 4 Kids USA, a shoe distribution project that blesses fatherless and underserved children in Orlando, Florida, and other cities, with new shoes, while keeping old shoes from going to landfills. Joshua and his wife, Deborah Ashley, reside in a suburb of Orlando with their two sons, twin daughters, and a daughter-in-law.